A Place in Time
Explicatus

Other Books by Darrett B. Rutman

John Winthrop's Decision for America

The Morning of America, 1603–1789

The Great Awakening: Event and Exegesis (editor)

American Puritanism: Faith and Practice

*Husbandmen of Plymouth: Farms and Villages of the
    Old Colony*

Winthrop's Boston: Portrait of a Puritan Town

The Old Dominion (editor)

A Militant New World, 1607–1640

With Anita H. Rutman

A Place in Time: Middlesex County, Virginia, 1650–1750

A Place in Time
Explicatus

DARRETT B. AND ANITA H. RUTMAN

———

W · W · NORTON & COMPANY

NEW YORK · LONDON

ISBN   0-393-01820-2

This book was produced by W. W. Norton & Company, Inc. from
camera-ready copy prepared by the authors using a North-
Star TM Advantage 8/16 microcomputer, FancyFont,TM
and an Epson MK-100III dot-matrix printer.

PUBLISHER'S NOTE

For the convenience of the reader *A Place in Time* has been published in two parts. The first, subtitled *Middlesex County, Virginia, 1650-1750*, is the primary volume. This volume constitutes a supplementary part and presents statistical evidence which underlies the narrative of the first. All references to chapters in the text and notes of this volume refer to the chapters of the primary volume.

PREFACE

Grey with their dust, cribbed in with facts
and dates,
On foundered centuries the historian waits.
Ashes in balance, he sifts, weighs, meditates.

Walter de la Mare
Winged Chariot

Historical research of any kind ulti-
mately involves the problem–solving art. In describing the evolving
web of relationships in Middlesex County, Virginia between 1650 and
1750 in the corpus of this work, published separately, we have for
the most part done as many historians do: tucked solutions to
particular problems into the narrative with just enough of the way
in which they were reached to lend credence to them but not so much
as might tend to detour the reader from the main point. But not
always.

On a number of points we have silently assumed answers without
even stipulating problems. We have, for example, dealt with our
subject in the context of high mortality, the rapid and almost
inevitable remarriage of widows and widowers, and slow but steady
natural growth. Each of these, however, is problematic rather than

certain. In other instances a problem has been inferred and the solution offered in terms of selected vignettes—the network of friends and kin in which, from the beginning, the families of Middlesex were enmeshed, for example, or the declining position of the lower and middling families as slavery settled on the county. But that the vignettes point to the central tendency of the society is simply implied, not demonstrated.

The omissions have not been inadvertent. Problems of this kind require statistical solutions, the proper presentation of which sometimes involves an elaborate consideration of data and method. And because Chesapeake scholarship of the last decade or so has been commendably cumulative, solutions have frequently had to be arrived at (or placed within) the context of that scholarship. To us, the interruption of the narrative with such excursions has seemed an unwise departure from one of Clio's primary canons—that history in the last analysis is a literary art. We have, therefore, grouped what would otherwise be interruptions into this series of *explicatus*. The conclusions reached in the various sections that follow have affected the narrative of the primary volume throughout but each is an independent entity and the whole set is ordered so as to conform roughly with the order in which particular issues first arise in the text, hence can be read by way of counterpoint. One assumption is implicit: That before entering upon these *explicatus* the reader has become familiar with the description of the data base in the preface and first chapter of *A Place in Time: Middlesex County Virginia, 1650–1750*—the primary volume of this work.

Our rules with regard to the partial modernization of quotations and the standardization of the variant spellings of proper names remain those outlined in the preface of the first volume. As in that volume, too, we have simplified references to the manuscript materials of Middlesex and its parent county, Lancaster, in the Virginia State Library, Richmond by citing only the county, a keyword drawn from the Library's own finder list, and inclusive dates. The notes themselves follow immediately upon the end of each section.

An element of style should be noted. When, occasionally, we have stipulated particular computations we have deliberately used a form of notation drawn from computer programming rather than mathematics. Thus the computation

$$n \; \frac{R - D}{N}$$

is expressed as

$$((R - D) / N) * n.$$

One need only keep in mind that operations—viz.: addition (+), subtraction (−), multiplication (*), and division (/)—are performed in order from the interior parentheses outward. In the case of the example, the subtraction is performed before the division, which is performed before the multiplication. The form, we believe, has the advantage of clarity (once this principle is grasped) and economy.

D. B. R., A. H. R.

Durham, New Hampshire
August 1982

Contents

A Place in Time
Explicatus

one

TOBACCO PRICES

Modern research into the nature of
Chesapeake society began largely in Maryland materials hence conclusions regarding the Chesapeake as a whole were, and in the main
continue to be, extrapolations. But important differences between
colonies and even, within colonies, between regions, must be expected and accommodated in coming to conclusions, a fact that arrests
our attention immediately upon considering the materials of our
Virginia county. For by the end of the seventeenth century tobacco
prices in Middlesex differed radically from Maryland prices as
reported in a number of extensive price series compiled by various
historians.[1]

The Maryland series consist of mean annual tobacco prices per
pound as drawn from probate records, inventories, and accounts,
converted to sterling. Similar figures can be found in the records
of Middlesex and converted to sterling using rates from John J.
McCusker's *Money and Exchange in Europe and America*.[2] In
only four instances, however, and even then only barely in two, are
there enough data to establish a yearly figure. But in these years,
and when the data from Middlesex and Maryland are aggregated on a
decadal basis, the differential is clear. Table 1 summarizes.

TABLE 1

Middlesex and Maryland Tobacco Prices by Decade and
Select Years, 1670–1750, in Pence per Pound

Years	Middlesex			Maryland Sterling	Middlesex as % of Maryland
	N	Current	Sterling		
1670–1679	11	1.34	1.10	1.06	103.8
1680–1689	13	1.32	1.08	0.86	125.6
1690–1699	5	1.30	1.10	0.85	129.4
1700–1709	12	1.63	1.34	0.90	148.9
1700	6	1.68	1.38	1.00	138.0
1710–1719	21	1.70	1.40	1.03	135.9
1717	10	1.63	1.34	1.05	127.6
1720–1729	33	1.56	1.28	1.18	108.5
1727	11	1.55	1.27	1.13	112.4
1728	6	1.55	1.28	1.06	120.8
1730–1739	9	1.82	1.46	1.01	144.5
1740–1749	19	1.67	1.33	1.17	113.7

‖*Source & Notes:* Middlesex figures have been compiled from the records
of the county; Maryland figures 1650–1729 have been aggregated from Russell
R. Menard, "The Tobacco Industry in the Chesapeake Colonies, 1617–1730: An
Interpretation," *Research in Economic History,* V (1980), 157–161;
1730–1749 from Paul G.E. Clemens's Talbot County series reported in his *The
Atlantic Economy and Colonial Maryland's Eastern Shore,*
(Ithaca, N.Y., 1980), 225–227, converted to sterling. These particular Maryland
series were selected as reflecting in their generally higher price levels the
very best oronoco. The complexity of the monetary situation in Maryland
after 1733 makes the conversion to sterling in the last two decades question-
able but comparison of unconverted values shows much the same differential;
Middlesex prices averaged 136% of Talbot's in the 1730s, 108% in the 1740s.

To some extent the differential between Maryland and Middlesex
tobacco prices through the 1730s can be accounted for by the different
quality of tobacco exported, a point developed in the next section. But
the greater part of the difference would seem to lie in the fact that
different varieties of tobacco were grown in the areas covered. Middlesex was, by the last decade of the seventeenth century, devoted
almost exclusively to sweetscented tobacco, Maryland throughout the
period to oronoco, two varieties with quite distinct overseas markets
and quite different prices.

Until the 1660s oronoco was the standard tobacco of the Chesapeake. Sweetscented was a "new sort" in 1665 when Gloucester
County's Alexander Moray wrote of it to an English correspondent.[3]

The "new sort" entered what would become Middlesex very early, for in late 1664 in Lancaster County—Middlesex's parent county— the county court, in resolving a debt case, ordered that such tobacco "as shall appeare arronoake" be rated at ten shillings a hundred while arbitrators were to appraise the value of "that [which] shall appeare sweet sented."[4] Both varieties were common in the mid-1670s when, following the county's formation, John Burnham and Robert Beverley proposed to the Middlesex court that they supply arms to the county militia and be compensated at a rate of a penny a pound sweetscented or 0.67 pence a pound oronoco.[5] The early price differential reflected the early appearance of different markets. John Banister wrote in 1679 that the more aromatic and lighter tasting sweetscented had taken Englishmen by storm, that they "piped" it at a great rate while transshipping the harsher oronoco to the continent.[6] In Middlesex, where the soil was ideal for the former, sweetscented rapidly replaced oronoco.[7] Sellers, lessors, even the county court itself in assessing fines, were soon accepting only the sweetscented variety.[8] The timing of the shift can be seen in the Middlesex-Maryland price differentials reported in table 1. In the 1670s the two areas were about equal, but by the 1690s Middlesex tobacco prices were roughly 130 percent of Maryland prices while in the the first decade of the new century the differential neared 150 percent.

The rise and eventual fall of the price differential in table 1 hints at the market conditions of the two varieties and of the economic fortunes of planters tied to one or the other. The series for Maryland (oronoco) reflects what scholarship has been depicting recently for the Chesapeake in general: slowly falling prices through the greater part of the seventeenth century, an abrupt drop in the 1680s when supply finally glutted the market, a long depression broken only by a short-run recovery in the late 1690s and early 1700s, the depressed prices recovering gradually in the early decades of the eighteenth century, tumbling again in the late 1720s, and climbing rapidly from about 1735 as British merchants developed extensive new markets for tobacco in France and the Netherlands. But the Middlesex series (sweetscented) shows a quite different course.

On the one hand, planters moving to sweetscented in the 1660s and 1670s were spared the price collapse of the 1680s. Their pro- duct was in the process of capturing the English market. Indeed, the availability of sweetscented tobacco in quantity might well have been an additional depressant on oronoco prices. Moreover, there was a limit to which the sweetscented supply could grow inasmuch as the variety had a restricted geographic range in the Chesapeake. While oronoco would grow anywhere, sweetscented prospered only on the peninsulas between the James and Rappahannock rivers, an area largely settled and in production by 1700. In consequence, the price reached in the the first decade of the new century could not break by virtue of oversupply.

On the other hand, the sweetscented price had no place to go when, at the end of the period, the oronoco price shot upward. Sweetscented planters supplied an essentially inelastic market; if there was a trend in demand at all it was a downward movement setting in during the 1720s as Englishmen took to the better grades of oronoco.[9] Saved depressed prices at one end of the series, in other words, the sweetscented planters were denied the price increase accruing to oronoco at the other.

|●|

1. Russell R. Menard, "The Tobacco Industry in the Chesapeake Colonies, 1617–1730: An Interpretation," *Research in Economic History*, V (1980), 157–161; Paul G. E. Clemens, *The Atlantic Economy and Colonial Maryland's Eastern Shore: From Tobacco to Grain* (Ithaca, 1980), 225–227; Carville V. Earle, *The Evolution of a Tidewater Settlement System: All Hallow's Parish, Maryland, 1650–1783* (Chicago, 1975), 228–229. Menard's series extends from 1616 through 1730 but encompasses his own research in Maryland and Virginia materials only through 1658 and in Maryland materials alone through 1719; he draws from Clemens for the period 1720–1730. Clemens's series are constructed from probate materials from Talbot County (1680–1772) and Kent County (1720–1775); as he reports, he did not include "listings for trash or debt tobacco." Earle's series is drawn from Anne Arundel and Prince George's counties, 1711–1775 and obviously includes trash. Earle's series, an earlier version of Menard's 1616–1658 figures, and his 1659–1710 figures are included in U.S. Bureau of the Census, *Historical Statistics of the United States, Colonial Times to 1970, Part 2* (Washington, D.C., 1975), 1198. All of these series apply exclusively to oronoco tobacco but where they overlap they show variations in yearly values. When decadal means are computed, for example, Menard's values are consistently a bit higher than Clemens's which are consistently well above those reported by Earle. This last discrepancy could well be the result of Clemens's exclusion and Earle's inclusion of trash tobacco which, together with ground leaves and seconds, Earle estimated at just under half the crop.

2. John J. McCusker, *Money and Exchange in Europe and America, 1600–1775: A Handbook* (Chapel Hill, N.C., 1978), 205–212. It is clear from internal evidence of the records that Middlesex was using a customary exchange of 1.2155 sterling

to 1.0 Virginia through roughly 1728 and 1.25 thereafter.

3. "Letters Written by Mr. Moray, A Minister to Sr. R. Moray, From Ware River in Mockjack Bay, Virginia, Feb. 1, 1665," *William and Mary Quarterly*, 2d Ser., II (1922), 158. The earliest mention of sweetscented we have found is in *A Description of the Province of New Albion*. . . (London, 1648) in Peter Force, comp., *Tracts and Other Papers, Relating Principally to the*. . . *Colonies in North America* (Washington, D.C., 1836-1847), II, Tract VII, 25-26.

4. Lancaster Orders, 1655-1666, 314.

5. Middlesex Orders, 1673-1680, 7.

6. Joseph and Nesta Ewan, eds., *John Banister and His Natural History of Virginia, 1678-1692* (Urbana, Ill., 1970), 41. See also "An Account of the Indians in Virginia [1689]," ed. Stanley Pargellis, *WMQ*, 3d Ser., XVI (1959),238.

7. John Clayton discussed the appropriate soils for the two in 1688. Edmund Berkeley and Dorothy Smith Berkeley, eds., *The Reverend John Clayton: A Parson With a Scientific Mind. His Scientific Writings and Other Related Papers* (Charlottesville, Va., 1965), 63.

8. See for example lease of Patrick Miller to James Grundy and Robert Gleave, August 13, 1681, and William Churchill to John Sibley, October 7, 1699, Churchill Family Papers, 1666-1777, Alderman Library, University of Virginia, Charlottesville, Va.; Middlesex Orders, 1673-1680, 167; 1680-1694, 6; 1694-1705, 28; Middlesex Deeds, 1679-1694, 182.

9. Clemens, *Atlantic Economy*, 29-39, 112 succinctly describes the oronoco price history. Arthur Pierce Middleton, *Tobacco Coast: A Maritime History of Chesapeake Bay in the Colonial Era* (Newport News, Va., 1953), 97-99 notes the decline in the sweetscented market. See also Jacob M. Price, *France and the Chesapeake: A History of the French Tobacco Monopoly, 1674-1791* (Ann Arbor, Mich., 1973), I, 667-668. We have no sense of the boom and bust cycles in sweetscented prices similar to those which Maryland scholars have reported for oronoco. Equally to the point, an attempt to validate the existence of cycles with a sophisticated econometric analysis using data offered to confirm their existence fails. (Personal communication to the authors from Charles Wetherell, University of California, Riverside.)

two

TOBACCO PRODUCTIVITY

How productive was one laborer in the
tobacco fields of the Chesapeake? The question admits of no easy
answer.

The problem can be addressed, first, on the level of the entire
society. We have, for the period after 1670, reasonably strong
figures for the number of pounds of tobacco exported annually from
the Chesapeake to England and, after the Act of Union of 1707,
Scotland. If we assume that, relative to these annual totals, the
amount of tobacco consumed locally or exported illegally was minimal, the exports offer a reasonable approximation of the size of the
crop. We have, too, rough decadal estimates of the total population
of the Chesapeake.The simple division of population into the size
of the crop offers us the time series of pounds tobacco per person
depicted on the accompanying figure. By this measure productivity
in the region seems to have held fairly constant (350 to 400 pounds
per person) during the last decades of the seventeenth century
but dropped steadily through the early decades of the eighteenth,
dipping under 150 pounds per person in 1750. Unfortunately, however,
the series measures the changing nature of the population more
than it measures the productivity of the laborer. We know that in

the seventeenth century the number of white male servants imported for the specific purpose of laboring in the fields was proportionately large and the number of women and children proportionately small. The downward trend in productivity depicted reflects in large measure the redress of this balance.

FIGURE 1

Chesapeake Trends in Tobacco Productivity
per Tithable and per Person, 1670-1750

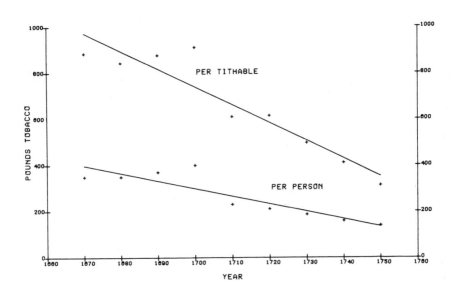

‖*Source and Notes*: Data from Gloria L. Main, "Maryland and the Chesapeake Economy, 1670-1720," in Aubrey C. Land, et al., eds., *Law, Society and Politics in Early Maryland* (Baltimore, Md., 1977), 134, 137, with Main's tobacco per tithables extended using U.S. Bureau of the Census, *Historical Statistics of the United States, Colonial Times to 1970, Part 2* (Washington, D.C., 1975), 1189-1190, and Evarts B. Greene and Virginia D. Harrington, comps., *American Population Before the Federal Census of 1790* (New York, 1932), 139-140, extrapolating where necessary. In the absence of figures for 1670 and 1680, Main's figures for 1673 and 1682 have been used. 1690 has been derived by linear extrapolation. Trend lines are least squares estimates defined by $Y^* = 972 - (77.5 * X)$ (per tithable), $Y^* = 397.9 - (33.0 * X)$ (per person), where Y^* is a trend value, X the elapsed time in 10 year intervals from 1670.

To minimize the effect of a changing population, historian Gloria L. Main attacked the problem of productivity by shifting the denominator of the calculation from the size of the total population to the size of the labor force, defining the laboring force as the Virginians and Marylanders themselves did for purposes of taxation, that is, the number of tithables: all white males above fifteen years of age and blacks of both sexes above that age.[1] The results are also shown on figure 1.

Again there seems to have been a constant level of productivity through the last decades of the seventeenth century and a steady decline in the eighteenth. But again we are probably not measuring simply the productivity of the tobacco laborer. We know that as the eighteenth century progressed more and more laborers (both white and black) were at work elsewhere than in the tobacco fields. Other crops—wheat in particular—were becoming important, in some areas of Virginia and Maryland more important than tobacco. And even in tobacco areas large segments of the labor force were withdrawn from the fields. In the 1720s Virginia's legislature attempted to define the tobacco laborer by specifically citing those who were not to be so considered. The list was long and included masters of families with more than eight tithable servants or slaves working in tobacco; servants or slaves who worked at a trade on their master's plantation at any time between April 1 and September 1, or who worked at a trade at any time on the plantation of a person other than the master; and any servant or slave who, between the same two dates, was employed as a coachman, groom, waiting man, cook, dairymaid, or domestic.[2] To some extent, therefore, what looks like declining tobacco productivity in the figure is in reality a measure of the diversification of the economy and the increasing prosperity of the few would could afford grooms, coachmen, and maids.

Macro-measures—productivity per person or per tithable—have their uses but they do not answer the original question: How productive was one laborer in the tobacco fields of the Chesapeake. Travel accounts, diaries, and letters sometimes speak directly to the point. Thus in 1732 William Hugh Grove described "a Slaves task" as 6,000 plants of tobacco, ultimately making 1,000 pounds, plus work in the corn fields.[3] The problem with such figures is that they vary so widely. Lewis Cecil Gray, for example, listed fourteen estimates ranging from 400 to 4,000 pounds per laborer per year, leading Russell R. Menard to assume productivity of 1,500 to 2,000 pounds.[4] Edmund S. Morgan reviewed Gray's collection of estimates, added more, and looked at hiring rates and legal judgments, arguing that a laborer hired by the year for 1,500 pounds tobacco or an award of 1,500 as compensation for the loss of a servant's labor for a year implies that an individual could make a crop at least as large. But hiring rates and judgments also varied. Equally to the point when dealing with a society in which tobacco was used as currency, such figures were meant as reimbursement for *all* labor—including that in corn fields and with cattle—not just labor in the tobacco fields. Ultimately Morgan, although concluding that 1,500 pounds a year was as good an estimate as any, simply abandoned the effort to establish productivity on the grounds that it "undoubtedly varied with the quality of land used, the length of time it had been in use, the time spent in weeding and worming, the type of tobacco grown, and most of all, with the weather."[5] True enough. But the notion of variance is a fact of statistical life, and productivity is a statistic—the mean output per unit of labor —which we need.

Let us return to Grove's estimate of the slave's task as 6,000 plants. Grove was a traveler who spent a few months in Virginia in the early 1730s; he was reporting not personal experience but what he saw and heard during his brief stay. On one level his report of productivity in terms of number of plants is distinctly odd. Nobody else wrote in such terms, being content to note pounds of the finished product in the hogshead. On another level, however, plants per laborer is very much to be expected of Grove for it was a way of looking at productivity in vogue during his stay. Twice in the 1720s—in 1723 and again in 1728—the Virginia legislature attempted to regulate tobacco production by specifying the maximum number of plants which the laborer could tend. The key number was 6,000, the maximum established in both acts for the tithable laboring in tobacco. Males above the age of 10 and under 16 were limited to 3,000 plants; single householders without servants or slaves, and widows and the "femme sole" with but one tithable were allowed 10,000 plants.[6] Obviously these acts, or rather the assumptions behind them, are the source of Grove's account.

Two assumptions are inherent in the acts, the first quite explicitly stated in that of 1723. The laws did not involve a "stint" —a curtailment of production in order to raise the price. They specifically involved the quality of the finished product. "The

Merchants in Great Britain" had been complaining; they had
"given up great Quantites of Tobacco to be burnt by reason of the
meaness and bad handling thereof"; this had diminished the king's
revenue and, more importantly, diminished the planters' profit inasmuch
as the merchants were not paying for tobacco which went up in smoke
in just this fashion. The "Frauds and Mischiefs" which gave rise to
the situation were, moreover, traceable directly back to the tobacco
fields, to "the Planting on Land not proper for producing good
Tobacco and greater Crops than the persons employed therein are
able duly to tend."[7] The laws did not—perhaps could not—deal with
the first by prohibiting growing tobacco on inferior land; they only
addressed the latter, specifying an ideal level of productivity given
the quality of the product desired. The legislators, men who owed
their position largely to their success in cultivating and marketing
the weed, seem to be telling us that to the extent the Virginia
planter set his laborer to tend above 6,000 plants per year, the
planter was hazarding inferior, eventually unmerchantable tobacco.

The second assumption emerges when we consider the separate
provisions for householders without servants or slaves and for
widows and the *femme sole*. What did the legislators have in mind?
On the one hand, they could have been proceeding from a knowledge
of a difference in kind between men working for themselves (the
housekeeper working his own tobacco, diligent and careful in his
own interest) and men working for a master (servants and slaves,
presumed indolent and careless). Assuming this difference, the
legislators were stipulating that the quality of 10,000 plants would
be acceptable from the former but not from the latter. On the
other hand, they could have been responding to altruism of a sort,
a feeling that the strict quality control inherent in the lower ratio
would work an undue hardship on the poorer sort. A certain
measure of quality, therefore, could be sacrificed to quantity to
cover such cases. In either event, the legislators were stipulating
a range in productivity: Acceptable quality was to be found
somewhere between productivity levels of 6,000 plants per laborer
and 10,000.

Obviously productivity as pounds tobacco in the hogshead—the
finished product—is related to the number of plants tended per
laborer. The more plants tended, the more pounds produced. But
plants tended is not the only operative variable. Any given number
of plants could be tended in such a way as to produce more or fewer

pounds of the finished product depending upon the quality sought. One does not read long in the tobacco laws of Virginia and Maryland without sensing the various tricks of the trade whereby quantity could be increased at the expense of quality. Suckers emerging from the roots of the topped plants could be left to grow. The leaves of the main plant would be a bit smaller as a result, but the suckers would grow into a second (and vastly inferior) crop. The dead and withered leaves from the base of the plant—ground leaves, as they were called—could be gathered as part of the crop rather than discarded. Similarly, stems, immature leaves, even twigs and bits of grass and weeds—collectively "trash"—could be packed into the hogshead, contributing to poundage at the expense of quality. We must not forget, however, that there was always a price differential between grades of tobacco, between top and second, prime and the barely merchantable. Every Chesapeake planter, consciously or unconsciously, on his own volition or in accordance with colony statutes, was attempting to optimize profit by optimizing a quantity/quality ratio; his productivity was not simply a matter of how many plants he could tend but how many he chose to tend, and in what fashion.

In his 1975 study of All Hallow's Parish, Maryland, Carville V. Earle undertook what was to that point the most extensive research on productivity. On the basis of probate inventories and accounts of estates for which he could establish the size of the crop and the size of the labor force, Earle reported pounds tobacco per laborer per year varying between 1,600 and 2,200, concluding that the mean laborer tended 10,000 plants to produce between 1,800 and 1,900 pounds of tobacco.[8] There are a number of problems with the data on which his results are based, some of which Earle himself noted. The crucial element is the estimate of the number of laborers working any particular crop. The free white laborer was not counted by Earle—the hired hand, the sharecropper or tenant who had paid in what was due the estate, thus adding to the tobacco on hand, but was not himself listed as part of the labor force, overseers in the case of estates using large numbers of slaves. (The necessity of adding an overseer for roughly every ten hands was a case of scale operating against economy of operation, not for it.) Moreover, Earle excluded the decedent as a laborer whenever the estate included more than two servants or slaves, an unrealistic assumption as to the economic level at which the farmer withdrew himself from the fields and confined his labor to management. And in no case did Earle include the possible labor of a wife and the very probable labor of children. A Middlesex case illustrates this last point. In 1726 Augustine Owen died; the subsequent inventory of his estate listed 4,414 pounds of tobacco and two black slaves, a male, Sharp, and Betty. On the basis of this inventory Earle would have computed production per laborer at 1,605 pounds.[9] But Augustine had living at home two sons, ages 15 and 23. Adding these to the labor force reduces productivity to 1,309. If his daughters still at home (ages 26 and 20) are included, productivity drops to 768. And if his wife worked in the fields, the figure sinks to 679. In sum, Earle might well underestimate the labor force, hence overestimate productivity.

Nonetheless, Earle's figures, when contrasted to figures from Middlesex, contribute significantly to the problem of productivity —if not to solve the problem, then to make it more complex by introducing once again the probability of regional variation. For a number of reasons Maryland's extant probate records are far better than those for Virginia. Thus Earle could find 142 cases through 1749 in which both crop and labor force could be established. The Middlesex records offer only 92, and when these are grouped by time periods, particular periods appear clearly under-represented. When, however, the Middlesex sample is treated in the same fashion as Earle's—that is, the labor force per estate is computed in exactly the same way, accepting the probability of an overestimate of productivity—it becomes clear that in Middlesex production per laborer was significantly under that of Earle's All Hallow's Parish. Where Earle's cases ranged from roughly 1,600 to 2,200 pounds per laborer per year, those from Middlesex ranged from lows of 200 and 300 to a high of just under 2,100; indeed, only 7 of the 92 Middlesex cases exceeded Earle's reported low of 1,600 pounds. And where Earle estimated a mean of between 1,800 and 1,900 pounds per laborer, the Middlesex data compute to a mean of just over 900 pounds. Moreover, the difference between Middlesex and All Hallow's was —as table 2 indicates—consistent across time.

The lower productivity per laborer in Middlesex relative to that found by Earle for All Hallow's is suggested by still another source. In January 1725 Lieutenant Governor Hugh Drysdale submitted a report to London summarizing "the Tobacco planted and Tended in

TABLE 2

Middlesex and All Hallow's Parish, Maryland
Tobacco Yields per Laborer, 1650-1750

Years	Middlesex		All Hallow's	
	N	Mean	*N*	Mean
Thru 1699	4	1207.2	34	1914.0
1700-1709	10	968.5	16	2239.2
1710-1719	11 .	880.7	23	1687.7
1720-1729	36	987.8	18	1612.8
1730-1739	6	601.9	23	1706.7
1740-1749	25	778.1	28	1863.4
1700-1749	88	886.3	108	1804.6

‖*Source and Notes*: Middlesex figures have been compiled
from the manuscript probate records of the county. All
Hallow's are from Carville V. Earle, *The Evolution of a
Tidewater Settlement System: All Hallow's Parish,
Maryland, 1650-1783* (Chicago, 1975), 27. The median
of the Middlesex, 1700-1749 set = 767.3; the standard
deviation = 408.2. Earle reports only means.

Virginia" during the previous year, the first in which the Tobacco
Act of 1723 was in effect. In the report he listed for each county
the number of tithables, tithables tending tobacco, boys allowed to
tend 3,000 plants, the number of plants tended, and of hogsheads of
oronoco and sweetscented produced for export .[10] The report,
however, cannot be used uncritically.

Drysdale's count of hogsheads for export is clearly suspect. We
do not know where he obtained his numbers. And when his total of
just under 35,000 hogsheads is converted to pounds the total makes
up 90 percent of all imports into Great Britain in 1725, leaving only
10 percent to come from Maryland and elsewhere, a figure that should
be closer to 25 or 30 percent.[11] Moreover, even if we assume
Drysdale's numbers are correct, it is apparent that we are dealing
with an abnormal year. The trend in Chesapeake tobacco exports
to Great Britain, 1700-1750 suggests that the size of the export crop
in 1725 should have been in the area of 40 million pounds; the actual
export that year was only 63 percent of this figure. (See figure 2.)

The provenance of that part of Drysdale's report dealing with the number of people tending tobacco and the number of plants is known. The act of 1723 itself stipulated how the tobacco counters were to be appointed in the various counties and the method by which the plants were to be counted, while two returns—from Richmond and King George—have been located.[14] No return exists from Middlesex but the records of the county show that the local authorities conformed even to the extent of fining Armistead Churchill for listing a young female black as of age to tend tobacco when she was not.[15] Most telling is the tithable figure for Middlesex in the report. Normally when the county was called upon to report tithables to the central government the county authorities under-counted, a phenomenon apparent whenever colony counts are compared to local counts. When the county numbered its tithables in order to raise money for local purposes its count was invariably higher (and presumably more accurate) than those sent to the colony capital; the latter, after all, would be used to establish the proportion of the colony levy the county must pay, and it was in the interest of all in the county to keep it as low as possible.[16] But the count of tithables in Drysdale's report accurately reflects the local count. The very unusualness of this correspondence suggests that the county authorities took the act and the request for numbers seriously and did their best.

Provenance alone gives us more confidence in that part of Drysdale's report dealing with tobacco plants and the numbers tending the crop. Additionally, the count of plants would seem to be immune to the effects of adverse weather. Drought would affect the the yield per plant but not the planting itself, while the actual count of plants in June antedated the destruction by the hurricane in August. When, moreover, plants are converted to yield by the normal ratio of six plants per pound, the normal crop from so many plants can be estimated, in this case at just over 31 million pounds, 78 percent of the export expected for 1725, leaving Maryland to account for 22 percent. Drysdale's count of plants, in other words, can be used to approximate a roughly normal crop for Virginia as a whole, or for any county. At the same time the labor force producing this crop can be approximated and standardized in such a way as to allow the computation of a productivity figure comparable to those computed from probate by counting each adult male as one, each adult female as three quarters, and each male 12 through

15 as one half.[17] Drysdale's report stipulates the number of "boys"
and total tithables working in the crop, while a census drawn from
the Middlesex biographies described in chapter 1 suggests that 24
percent of the latter were black females.[18] On the basis of tithables
working in tobacco (T) and "boys" (B) a standardized labor count (L)
can be established by:

$$(0.76 * T) + (0.75 * (0.24 * T)) + (0.5 * B).$$

To be on the safe side, however, we reduce the result by 10 percent
to account for misattributions such as that indicated by the prose-
cution of Churchill and a general confusion as to exactly how to
define a tithable working in tobacco addressed in the Tobacco Act
of 1728. An estimate of pounds tobacco produced per laborer can now
be obtained from the number of plants (P) by:

$$(0.167 * P) / L.$$

For Middlesex these computations result in a productivity
figure of 1,009 pounds (compared to a mean figure of 900 for all
92 cases drawn from the Middlesex probate and 989 for the decade
1720–1729). The highest figure computed for any Virginia county was
1,489 pounds (York), a figure below Earle's minimum case. And overall
Virginia productivity computes to only 851 pounds per laborer. Except
for Middlesex these results are certainly not definitive. Standardizing
the labor force of all Virginia by extrapolating from one county is a
hazardous procedure at best. But the figures clearly suggest that
Virginia's productivity as a whole was nowhere near that of Maryland
as estimated by Earle.[19]
What accounts for the substantial variation between Middlesex
in Virginia and All Hallow's Parish in Maryland?[20] The two did
not differ radically in soil quality or weather. They did, however,
differ in the variety of tobacco grown. Middlesex, as we saw in the
preceding section, grew the more aromatic (and more expensive)
sweetscented tobacco while All Hallow's was devoted to oronoco.
And we know that there were differences in the cultivation of the two.
Sweetscented was topped low, with only six to eight leaves left on
each plant. Oronoco was topped high so as to leave fourteen and more
leaves.[21] There is a hint that the difference led to a difference in
yield: the Reverend John Clayton recounted the complaint of a

Gloucester widow that tobacco grown in the rich soil of a drained swamp "produced so very large, that it was suspected to be of the Aranoko kind." But Clayton's advice—top down to four or five leaves and so make "more Tobacco, and less Leaves"—implies that the difference was a matter of foliage, not finished product. The fewer sweetscented leaves were each thicker and more compact than the many "light and chaffy" oronoco leaves, with the difference in heft cancelling the difference in numbers.[22] If there was any intrinsic difference in yield between varieties it was undoubtedly slight, certainly not enough to account for the great variation between Middlesex and All Hallow's.[23] And, of course, any difference between sweetscented and oronoco would not explain the disparity in productivity between All Hallow's and Virginia's oronoco counties, the latter far more in line with sweetscented Middlesex.

Earle himself offers the most important clue to the reason behind the different levels of productivity. Both Maryland and Virginia passed frequent laws to control the quality of tobacco. Until the mid-eighteenth century, however, Maryland's statutes were both fewer and less stringently enforced than those of Virginia.[24] Indeed, it seems a general assumption even at the time that a Maryland planter's crop would be a tenth to a quarter trash and up to a third seconds, while Earle's analysis of inventories indicates that trash, ground leaves, and seconds combined amounted to almost half the crop. When, in 1747, Maryland finally passed quality-control legislation with strong enforcement provisions, tobacco yields per laborer in All Hallow's abruptly dropped to 900 and 1,000 pounds —roughly the level found all along in Middlesex.[25] What this seems to point to is a regional difference in the Chesapeake. The All Hallow's planters were solving the problem of optimizing the quality/quantity ratio by sacrificing the former to the latter. They were setting their laborers to as many plants as possible, pressing as many pounds as possible from their plants, and accepting a lesser price for their larger crops. The Middlesex planters were proceeding in opposite fashion, accepting smaller crops of greater quality and commensurately higher prices. Drysdale's 1725 report, moreover, suggests that the Middlesex way was common throughout Virginia.

The data summarized in table 2 suggest still another point about productivity in Middlesex and All Hallow's parish. In examining productivity over time, Earle concluded that there was essentially

FIGURE 3

Middlesex and All Hallow's Parish, Maryland
Trends in Tobacco Productivity per Laborer,
1650-1750

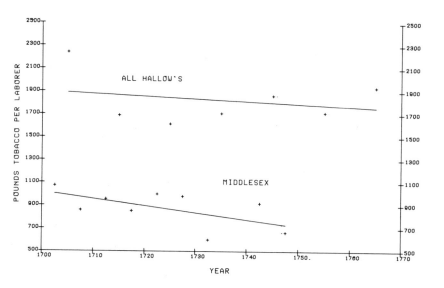

‖*Source and Notes*: Middlesex from manuscript probate records of the
county; All Hallow's from Carville V. Earle, *The Evolution of a Tidewater
Settlement System: All Hallow's Parish, Maryland, 1650-1783* (Chicago,
1975), 27. Extreme high and low values have been excluded from the Middlesex set
to minimize the danger of including partial inventories and erroneous labor counts;
with these values included the trend would be sharper. The trend lines are
least squares estimates and are defined as $Y^* = 1887.42 - (21.41 * X)$ where
X is the elapsed time in 10 year intervals from 1705 (All Hallow's) and
$Y^* = 1002.31 - (30.12 * X)$ where X is the elapsed time in 5 year intervals
from 1702.5 (Middlesex).

no change and made this conclusion a part of an argument against
soil exhaustion as a significant factor in the agriculture of his parish
and by extrapolation the Chesapeake.[26] Much of his argument as to
the prevalence of a long-term rotation system mitigating against
the exhaustive effect of tobacco culture holds true for Middlesex.
Using the very harshest of assumptions, for example, the Middlesex
ratio of land to labor would force the recultivation of tobacco old

fields roughly every 50 years, a figure well above the 20 years which would indicate an overtaxing of the land, above even All Hallow's 44 years.[27] But productivity in Middlesex—expressed as the mean pounds tobacco produced per laborer per year—did decline over the years. Figure 3 depicts the trend lines suggested by the Middlesex and All Hallow's data. Both are downward. The fit of the All Hallow's data to the trend is so poor as to deny significance, hence Earle was quite right in arguing that his data show no movement over time. The Middlesex data, however, are quite otherwise, the statistically significant trend line absorbing 36 percent of the variation.[28] As in the case of the data depicted in figure 1 we are not sure what is being measured by this decline. Earle's argument relative to soil exhaustion, applied to Middlesex, argues against a real decline in productivity—the laborer coaxing less and less tobacco from ever more exhausted fields. It seems far more likely that the trend reflects the changing nature of the labor force (from white servants—largely males in their late teens and early twenties—to prime black males, and, as described in a subsequent section, from prime blacks to a more normal black population) and to some extent an increasing assignment of blacks to tasks apart from the tobacco field as the eighteenth century progressed.

|●|

1. Gloria L. Main, "Maryland and the Chesapeake Economy, 1670–1720," in Aubrey C. Land, et al., eds., *Law, Society, and Politics in Early Maryland* (Baltimore, Md., 1977), 134–152.

2. Waverly K. Winfree, comp., *The Laws of Virginia: Being a Supplement to Hening's The Statutes at Large, 1700–1750* (Richmond, Va., 1971), 295–305.

3. Gregory A. Stiverson and Patrick H. Butler, III, eds., "Virginia in 1732: The Travel Journal of William Hugh Grove," *Virginia Magazine of History and Biography*, LXXXV (1977), 32.

4. Lewis Cecil Gray, *History of Agriculture in the Southern United States to 1860* (Washington, D.C., 1933), I, 218–219; Russell R. Menard, "From Servant to Freeholder: Status Mobility and Property Accumulation in Seventeenth Century Maryland," *WMQ*, 3d Ser., XXX (1973), 51.

5. Edmund S. Morgan, *American Slavery American Freedom: The Ordeal of Colonial Virginia* (New York, 1975), 142–143, 142n, 302.

6. Winfree, comp., *Supplement to Hening*, 247-253, 295-305.

7. Ibid., 247. Note that when, a century earlier, the number of plants had been limited in order to limit the size of the crop, the number of plants per laborer had been set at 3,000, 2,000, even 1,500. William W. Hening, comp., *The Statutes at Large: Being a Collection of All the Laws of Virginia from the First Session of the Legislature in 1619* (Richmond, Va., 1809-1823), I, 141-142, 152, 163, 188-190, 203-207.

8. Earle, *Evolution of a Tidewater Settlement*, 25-28. In her forthcoming study of Maryland, 1650-1720, Gloria Main estimates 1,500 pounds per laborer on the basis of 1,000 observations from the probate records of six counties of Maryland. Paul G. E. Clemens, "Economy and Society on Maryland's Eastern Shore, 1689-1733," Land, et al., eds., *Law. Society. and Politics in Early Maryland*, 156n found a differential range in production between single tenant farmers (1,000 to 2,100 pounds) and married tenants (1,500 to 4,000).

9. Counting adult males as one laborer, slave women as 0.75, and servant and slave boys, 12-15 , as .5, always excluding the aged, infirm, or decrepit.

10. "An Account of the Quantity of Tobacco Planted & Tended in Virginia in the Year 1724. . . ," C.O. 5/1319, 220, Public Record Office, London. Reported in *Journal of the Commissioners for Trade and Plantations* (London, 1920-1938), V, 195 as an enclosure with a letter from Drysdale of January 29, 1725. George Maclaren Brydon, *Virginia's Mother Church and the Political Conditions Under Which It Grew* (Richmond, Va., 1947-1952), 363-364 summarizes the report.

11. Converting to pounds tobacco using net weights of 600 and 700 pounds per hogshead oronoco and sweetscented respectively as set by the Virginia legislature in laws of 1713 and 1720. Winfree, comp., *Supplement to Hening*, 75-90, 185-191. On imports into Great Britain in 1725 see Price, *France and the Chesapeake*, II, 843. Maryland's share of the export was steadily dropping in the 18th century. Price might well be overstating Maryland's share (ibid., I, 668) but it was hardly a mere 10% in 1725.

12. The act and its successor act of 1728 were in force from 1725 through 1730. If they had effected a stint one would expect that exports during these years would reflect the fact by being consistently under the 1700-1750 trend. Three years were, three years were not, no deviation from the trend except that of 1725 is significant. When, moreover, semi-average trends are computed for the whole set 1700-1750 and for the set excluding 1725-1730, there is less than a 1% difference. In the first instance the trend is defined by $30562.05 + (791.21 * X)$, where X is an annual increment; in the second by $30781.4 + (796.93 * X)$. One would expect a greater difference if the crop of the five years had been purposefully and significantly stinted.

13. Virginia Colonial Records Project, "Survey Report," Nos. 414, p. 15; 245, p. 6; 849, Typescript, Virginia State Library, Richmond, David M. Ludlum, *Early American Hurricanes. 1492-1870* (Boston, 1963), 20-21.

14. William P. Palmer, et al., eds., *Calendar of Virginia State Papers and Other Manuscripts. [1652-1869]* (Richmond, Va., 1875-1893), I, 208. A third incomplete and misdated return is to be found in ibid., 68.

15. C. G. Chamberlayne, ed., *The Vestry Book of Christ Church Parish. Middlesex County. Virginia 1663-1767* (Richmond, Va., 1927], 202-203.

Middlesex Orders, 1721–1726, 165, R. T. Barton, ed., *Virginia Colonial Decisions: Reports by Sir John Randolph and Edward Barradall of Decisions of the General Court of Virginia 1728–1741* (Boston, 1909), R26–R30.

16. Darrett B. and Anita H. Rutman, "'More True and Perfect Lists': The Reconstruction of Censuses for Middlesex County, Virginia, 1668–1704," *Va. Mag. Hist. Biog.*, LXXXVIII (1980), 43, Darrett B. Rutman, "History Counts: or, Numbers Have More Than Face Value," *Reviews in American History*, IV (1976), 372–378.

17. See Note 9 above.

18. See Rutman and Rutman, "'More True and Perfect Lists,'" *Va. Mag. Hist. Biog.*, LXXXVIII (1980), 37–74 for the way in which Middlesex censuses have been reconstructed.

19. If Virginia's laboring force of 1725 had been producing at the rate Earle established for All Hallow's, Maryland (each laborer tending 10,000 plants to make a crop of between 1,800 and 1,900 pounds), the 1725 Virginia crop, barring drought and hurricane, would have been some 67 million pounds, a figure not reached by Virginia and Maryland *combined* until the late 1740s.

20. Earle does not report enough statistics from his distribution to allow a formal difference-of-means test, but that the samples reflect two different realities seems clear enough.

21. Ewan and Ewan, eds., *Banister*, 360–361. Other sources specify different numbers of leaves but all agree that sweetscented was tended with fewer.

22. Berkeley and Berkeley, eds., *Clayton*, 82, Ewan and Ewan, eds., *Banister*, 360.

23. A significant difference in yield would surely have left some imprint in either the literature or the law. We have found no hint other than Clayton's. Although the size of the finished crop reported by Drysdale is suspect and drought and hurricane would sharply affect the result, a computation of plants per pound from his report is suggestive: 8.17 oronoco, 8.37 sweetscented.

24. Gray, *Agriculture*, I, 224–231 summarizes.

25. Earle, *Evolution of a Tidewater Settlement*, 26, 98–99.

26. Ibid., 27–30, arguing against Avery Odelle Craven's classic *Soil Exhaustion as a Factor in the Agricultural History of Virginia and Maryland, 1606–1860* (Urbana, Ill., 1926).

27. In applying the computations suggested by Earle, *Evolution of a Tidewater Settlement*, 29, we have used the acreage patented rather than total acreage of the county, and the number of tithables augmented by 20% to account for non-tithables in the work force. Using Earle's more generous assumptions, the number of years to recultivation (computed for 1702, 1726, and 1750) would be over 100 in the first two instances, 67 in the third.

28. Significant at the 0.05 level.

three

POPULATION ESTIMATES

The reconstruction of demographic trends within Middlesex is essentially based upon three data sets: annual counts of the number of births drawn from the biographies described in chapter 1, annual counts of deaths similarly derived, and annual counts of the number of tithables actually made within the county for purposes of taxation. All three are summarized in figure 4, with births and deaths disaggregated into white and black.[1] Each set suggests important and unique information but each is defective in one fashion or another, hence their application to particular questions requires care both in the doing and in drawing conclusions.

The growth of population within the county is our first question. The annual count of tithables is immediately suggestive, but tithable counts are in general understatements. They are, moreover, subject to variation as the very definition of "tithable" changed. They seldom discriminate between white and black tithables, an important distinction to be made as the county shifted from white to black bound labor. And they do not in and of themselves tell us the *total* population at any point in time, only the number of individuals the society considered laboring, income-producing persons. The relationship between the number of tithables and the total population, while

FIGURE 4

Births, Deaths, and Tithables in Middlesex, 1650–1750

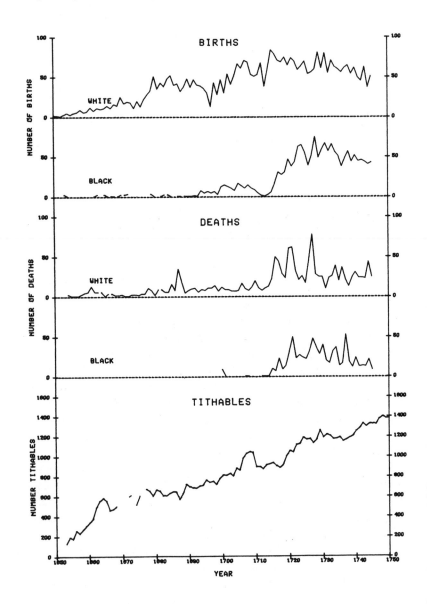

||*Source:* See text. Missing and zero values are not plotted.

estimated by any number of scholars, remains uncertain.[2]

We have attempted to cope with these problems by first extracting from the biographies those persons known to be in the county at particular points in time, comparing the number of such known individuals with contemporary estimates of the population to isolate those groups more likely than others to have been missed in the record-stripping process underlying the biographies, and compiling a series of pseudo-censuses. This elaborate procedure—a matter of adjusting raw categorical counts by weighting for the number in each category that we estimate missing—together with its testing, has been fully described elsewhere.[3] Suffice it to say here that the "reconstructed censuses" prove remarkably strong reflections of the reality and supply us with a number of vital parameters, including growth rates by race and the changing ratios of the number of blacks to total population and of total population to tithables. These parameters, reported in table 3, offer us in turn effective benchmarks when we address the question of population and population change in the interstitial years between censuses.

We begin with the assumption that there were linear shifts in the ratios of black to total population and of total to tithables between one census point and another, hence the ratios for any particular year can be arrived at by simple extrapolation, viz.:

$$((R2 - R1) / N) * n$$

where R1 and R2 are the ratios at any two censuses, R1 being the earlier, N the number of years between the two, and n the number of years elapsed from the earlier census to the year for which we are estimating.[4] However, the two resulting series of ratios (total population to tithables and blacks to total) cannot be applied directly to the raw data. There are some years for which we have no tithable counts, while in the early years a dip in the number of tithables in 1657 and a "nose" jutting up from the general trend in the years 1662-1665—both obvious in figure 4—seem more artifacts of the shifting definition of who was tithable than reflections of population changes.[5] From the mid-1680s, moreover, black slaves began arriving directly from Africa in ever-larger numbers, a fact compounding our problem in two ways. First, the blacks did not arrive at a steady rate but in groups as individual slave ships disgorged their cargoes either in Middlesex or near enough to the county that

TABLE 3

The Population of Middlesex as Reconstructed for
Specific Points in Time

Year	Population		Ratios		Annual Change (%)		
	White	Non- white	Non- white to Total	Total to Tith- ables	White	Black	Both
1668	847	65	0.07	1.81	37.5	23.2	37.9
1687	1337	117	0.08	2.34	2.4	3.1	2.5
1699	1374	397	0.22	2.29	0.2	10.2	1.6
1704	1436	553	0.29	2.29	0.9	6.6	2.3
1724	1423	1293	0.50	2.33	-0.1	4.2	1.6
1740	1348	1596	0.54	2.34	-0.3	1.3	0.5

‖*Source and Notes*: Censuses reconstructed from the Middlesex prosopography by the method described in Darrett B. and Anita H. Rutman, "'More True
and Perfect Lists': The Reconstruction of Censuses for Middlesex County, Virginia,
1668-1704," *Virginia Magazine of History and Biography*, LXXXVIII
(1980), 37-74. The numbers here differ from those reported earlier in the addition
of censuses of 1724 and 1740 and a refinement of that of 1668. The annual
percent change is computed following George W. Barclay, *Techniques of
Population Analysis* (New York, 1958), 31-32. The year 1650 is arbitrarily
established as the starting point for the population and assigned a population
of 1 in computing the annual percent change 1650-1668.

Middlesex planters could make purchases.[6] Second, the arriving
blacks axiomatically shifted the ratios of population to tithables and
blacks to total away from their general trends, at least for a few
years. The point is easily illustrated: Assume that in a given year
there were 1,000 tithables, a ratio of population to tithables of 2.5
and of black to total of 0.075—that is, the population numbered 2,500
in all with 188 blacks. Assume, too, the arrival of a slave ship with
115 blacks. Given what we know of the demographic characteristics of
such cargoes it is not unrealistic to assume that 100 of the arriving
blacks would be immediately tithable, hence the tithable count would
jump to 1,100. If at this point we were to apply the ratios of 2.5 and
0.075 we would estimate a total population of 2,750 with 206 blacks,
but in reality the population would have grown only to 2,615 and there
would be 303 blacks.The true ratios would have shifted to 2.38 and
0.116. But both ratios would shift rapidly back toward their trend
lines, in some measure because of births to arriving black women in-

creasing the number of non-tithables, in greater part because of extraordinarily high mortality among the newly arrived blacks.[7]

In the face of missing data, meanders in the tithable count attributable to changes in the law rather than changes in the population, and radical variations in the count as slave ships arrived, estimating the characteristics of the population between census years becomes more complicated than a simple application of extrapolated ratios to the number of tithables. The missing tithable counts (for 1669–1671, 1673, and 1676) have been estimated by distributing equally the gain or loss between known years. The meanders of 1652 and 1662–1665 have been graphically smoothed. (The bulge in 1706–1710, however, cannot be accounted for by a change of law hence remains untouched.) And we have adjusted for sudden influxes of new blacks, our method being to account sharp upward deviations from the trend in the number of tithables after 1680 as newly arrived, tithable blacks and dissipate the impact of their arrival over the subsequent years. Thus if T represents the expected number of tithables in any given year assuming a linear trend between censuses, G a sharp upward deviation from the trend value, and RT and RB the extrapolated ratios of total to tithables and blacks to total respectively, we have assumed the population (P) of that year to be

$$(T * RT) + G.$$

The population black to be

$$((P - G) * RB) + G.$$

And the population white to be

$$P - B.$$

The dissipation of the influx has been accomplished by applying the same computation over the succeeding three years but with G sequentially halved.[8] And throughout, the adjustments have been constrained by the reconstructed censuses themselves, for at each census year all values have been brought into correspondence with the reconstructions, thereby limiting any cumulative effect flowing from erroneous assumptions. Figure 5 presents the results of these computations, a graphic illustration of the rapidity with which the county grew,

FIGURE 5

Estimated Population of Middlesex by Year,
1653–1750

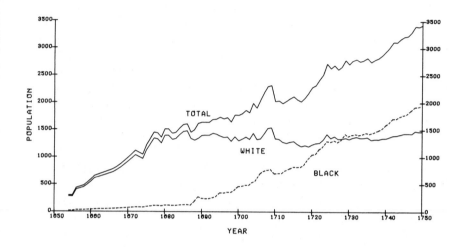

||*Source*: See text.

the relatively sudden advent of a black laboring force, and the con-
sequent decline of the white population.

Beyond affording such an illustration, the computations—or,
rather, the numbers computed—allow us to take the analysis one step
further. The numbers represent our best estimate of the population of
the county by race in any given year, specifically the mid–year population given that they are based upon tithables and that the tithables
were counted in the summer or early fall. We also have a count of the
number of births and deaths known to have occurred in the county
each year. In theory, therefore, we have the wherewithal to establish
crude birth and death rates and investigate the way in which the
population changed year by year. Births less deaths constitute the net
natural increase (or decrease), that is, the extent to which the
population gained or lost by virtue of the ability of its people to

procreate. The difference between net natural increase (or decrease) and real population growth (or loss) constitutes net migration—the extent to which the population changed by virtue of attracting newcomers (immigration) or suffering departures (emigration). Unfortunately there is a gap between theory and practice, for however much we know about births and deaths we know that we know too little, that the numbers we have (those depicted in figure 4) are undercounts, and that the degree of undercounting varied radically across time, worse in the earlier years, better (but never perfect) in the later years.

Once again we have applied to the reconstructed censuses. Using these we are able to make reasonably good estimates of the crude birth and death rates, in the case of birth rates for the census years themselves, in the case of death rates for the years between censuses in the aggregate. The rates computed from the censuses have been compared to rates computed using the appropriate raw counts of births and deaths and mid-year populations. The ratio between the two results, viz.,

$$E1 / E2$$

where E1 is a rate estimated from the census and E2 a rate estimated from the raw data, indicated the extent of the error of the latter.[9] Assuming a linear progression from bad to better counts, we extrapolated to find an error factor for each year and computed for each a first estimate of the crude birth and death rate. Visual inspection of the results quickly showed where the method failed. Erratic and more often than not missing black data for the years prior to 1700 vitiated any attempt to estimate black rates for the early years. Even for the years 1700–1715 our information on black deaths proved so inadequate as to defy correction, hence we resorted to a strategy (poor at best) of using white death rates increased by 10 percent. For the rest, visual inspection showed occasional failures which could be rectified. Yearly birth rates in the 30–35 per 1,000 range abruptly interrupted by a dip to 8 or 10 followed by recovery to 30–35 indicated a gross departure from the error trend assumed, one to be rectified by graphic smoothing. The resultant corrected series of crude birth and death rates were then used to compute the yearly series of net natural gains (or losses) depicted in figure 6.

The computation of net migration as a rate posed a conceptual

FIGURE 6

Estimated Net Natural Increase or Decrease
of the Middlesex Population by Year

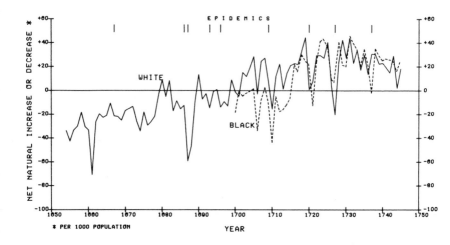

‖*Source:* See text.

problem in addition to the problems of data already discussed. Births
and deaths took place within a calendar year and rates could be computed on the basis of a mid-year population estimated from tithables.
Population change, however, given the nature of the data, was a
change from mid-year to mid-year, that is, from the point at which
tithables were counted in one year to the same point in the next, a
"tithable year," so to speak. It would have been inappropriate,
therefore, to attempt a direct computation of net migration (M) in
the classic fashion:

$$M = P2 - P1 - B + D$$

where P2 and P1 are the populations in successive years (P1 being the
earlier), B and D the intervening births and deaths. If the year in
question were 1700, P2 could only be the mid-year population of 1701
(roughly that of June 15) and P1 the population 12 months earlier. We

had no other numbers to supply. Yet the births (B) and deaths (D) occurred between January 1, 1700 and December 31, 1701; half of them really applied to the population change between June 1699 and June 1700, half to the change between June 1700 and June 1701. There were several possible ways to resolve this problem of calendar versus tithable year but the easiest way was to forget about the latter entirely, assume a linear growth between one June and the other, and set the population on any January 1 as the average between two Junes. The computation of net migration then involved three mid-year populations, those, for example, of 1699, 1700, and 1701. Our notation changes to reflect the more complex situation: Let P[x] be the mid-year population of any year x, P[x-1] the mid-year population of the prior year, and P[x+1] the mid-year population of the following year, then M[x]— that is, the net migration for year x—will be

$$((P[x] + P[x+1]) / 2) - ((P[x-1] + P[x]) / 2) - B + D.$$

Net migration as a rate per thousand follows as

$$(M[x] / P[x]) * 1000.$$

The resultant series is depicted in figure 7.

There are no real surprises in these last two figures. For a decade scholars have assumed (and perhaps made too much of the fact) that the early Chesapeake was a demographic disaster, that the number of deaths exceeded the number of births and the population grew largely by virtue of continuing immigration, a situation that changed only toward the end of the century. The figures confirm this overall picture, although it ought to be kept in perspective. There were more deaths than births, very simply, because there were more immigrants entering and hazarding death than there were women at risk of childbirth. This does not mean that had the immigrants stopped coming the population would have dwindled away—"expired" is the word one historian has used. The women already on hand would have continued to have children and some of these would have grown to maturity and had still more children, edging the population ever upward. Indeed, this is what happened when the immigrants *did* stop coming.[10]

Beyond confirming the overall picture, however, the first of the two figures underscores a truism about premodern populations such as

FIGURE 7

Estimated Migration into and out of
the Middlesex Population by Year

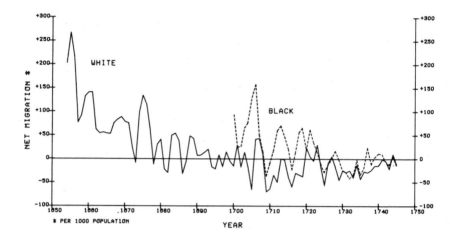

‖*Source:* See text.

that of Middlesex which other analyses have tended to obscure: the
enormous yearly variation.[11] Across the top of figure 6 we have
inserted markers to indicate years in which disease of one sort or
another was so rampant as to find lodgement in the literary evidence
from the period, an April 1688 memorandum concerning Virginia's
House of Burgesses, for example, that noted "A fast for the great
mortality. . .the people dyed, 1688, as in a plague," or a proclamation
of April 21, 1727: "Whereas the Inhabitants of this Colony have for
divers months past been visited with a violent sickness and very great
mortality. . . ."[12] The ability to isolate and measure these "public
calamities" makes the effort to go beyond aggregation and see yearly
variation worthwhile.

1. For purposes of analysis the handful of Indians and mulattos identified have been subsumed in the category "Black." The tithable count has been taken from the county rather than colony records, the latter almost invariably an understatement of the former. See Rutman and Rutman, "'More True and Perfect Lists,'" *Va. Mag. Hist. Biog.* LXXXVIII (1980), 42-48, and Rutman, "History Counts," *Rev. in Amer. Hist.*, IV (1976), 372-378. *The Parish Register of Christ Church, Middlesex County, Va. from 1653 to 1812* (Richmond, Va., 1897), a major source of births and deaths, ends abruptly in the late 1740s, hence the series depicted is foreshortened.

2. Morgan, *American Slavery American Freedom*, 395-405 is the best approach. Ours is a variation and extension of his.

3. In Rutman and Rutman, "'More True and Perfect Lists,'" *Va. Mag. Hist. Biog.*, LXXXVIII (1980), 37-74.

4. In extrapolating tithable ratios backward from the earliest census (1668) and forward from the latest (1740) we have used Morgan's 1640 ratio of 1.65 (*American Slavery American Freedom*, 404) and a 1755 ratio of 2.52 estimated for Middlesex by Robert E. and B. Katherine Brown, *Virginia 1705-1786: Democracy or Aristocracy?* (East Lansing, Mich., 1964), 72. The Browns also offer a 1755 black to total ratio by which we can extrapolate our black to total ratios 1740-1750. Our black to total ratio 1650-1667 is obtained by extending backward the 1668-1687 trend.

5. In 1657, precipitating the dip, Lancaster County arbitrarily struck black women from the tithable list and set out to compensate those who "have beene for many yeres past overcharged by retorneinge their Negroe Woemen in the list." The action was overturned by the colony government in 1662 but rather than simply restating an old law which had held black women tithable, the legislature provided a new law which specified all women laboring in the crop, by implication including as tithable for the first time white female servants and even some wives! The Lancaster Court seems to have held to the letter of the law for a few years, then retreated to what was obviously its spirit (all black women), hence the nose. Lancaster Orders, 1655-1666, 36, Hening, comp., *Statutes at Large*, II, 170.

6. The difficulties of a planter buying from afar are illustrated in William Fitzhugh's correspondence with Ralph Wormeley in 1681 and John Jackson in 1683. Richard Beale Davis, ed., *William Fitzhugh and His Chesapeake World, 1676-1701: The Fitzhugh Letters and Other Documents* (Chapel Hill, N.C., 1963), 93, 104, 127-128. A lesser planter would have had even more difficulty making such purchases.

7. On the characteristics of slave cargoes and the mortality of newly arrived blacks see particularly Allan Kulikoff, "A 'Prolific' People: Black Population Growth in the Chesapeake Colonies, 1700-1790," *Southern Studies* XVI (1977), 391-428.

8. We restricted the adjustment to upward deviations from the trend greater than 4% through 1724 and 1.6% thereafter, the latter to compensate for a steady decline in the white population discerned in other evidence. The justification for equating such upward deviations as marks of mass slave arrivals lies in the correlation of such with (1) literary evidence of the arrival of slave ships and (2) the appearance in the court records of relatively large numbers of age adjudgments of young, untithable blacks. The general configuration of slave

arrivals over time fits Kulikoff, "'Prolifick' People," *South. Stud.*, XVI (1977), 392–396, and Herbert S. Klein, "Slaves and Shipping in Eighteenth-Century Virginia," *Journal of Interdisciplinary History*, V (1975), 383–412.

9. The census birth and death rates are to be found in Rutman and Rutman "'More True and Perfect Lists,'" *Va. Mag. Hist. Biog.*, LXXXVIII (1980), 63, 65–66&n. Family reconstitutions allow the computation of an error rate and correction factor on a five year basis for births. See below, our discussions of "Mortality" and "Fertility." The magnitude and trend correspond to the annual error estimates computed here.

10. Morgan, *American Slavery American Freedom*, 180. See infra under "Fertility" for estimates of intrinsic rates of increase.

11. See e.g. E. A. Wrigley, *Population and History* (New York, 1969), 62–63.

12. Wyndham B. Blanton, *Medicine in Virginia in the Seventeenth Century* (Richmond, Va., 1930), 56, H. R. McIlwaine and W. L. Hall, eds., *Executive Journals of the Council of Colonial Virginia. 1680–1754* (Richmond, 1925–1945), IV, 129.

individual for whom no date of death was known was presumed to
have died the day after he last appeared in their records. The low
mortality estimate followed from the assumption that such an
individual lived for ten years after his last appearance and died
according to a mortality rate for his then-age derived from those
subjects whose date of death they knew. The true life expectancies
for various ages lay between these two extremes. Walsh and Menard's
unique contribution to the techniques of early American demographic
history was their way of distributing the unknown deaths to best
approximate the true values. In their method, unknowns were assumed
to have lived until the day after they last appeared in the records
alive, then died according to the mortality schedule established by
using known deaths alone. By way of example: Walsh and Menard,
using known deaths, established a figure of 23.3 years-left-to-live
for native-born males achieving age 20; a native-born male whose
death was unknown, last appearing alive at age 20, would be presumed
to have died at age 20+23.3 or in his 44th year, and his death
would be used in the computation of a "preferred" estimate of the
true life table values. But only to an extent.

In their first attempt to cast a life table using the method
described to this point, Walsh and Menard encountered what they
construed to be a "puzzling" anomaly.[2] They did not report the nature
of the anomaly in their published work but we can replicate their
procedure using data from Middlesex—specifically 394 males born
in Virginia between 1650 and 1699, 121 of whom disappeared from the
record base without leaving a precise date of death. The results are
depicted in the upper segment of figure 8. Note that rather than
consistently bounding discreet intervals, the high and low mortality
estimates converge and at one point at the higher ages even cross.
And rather than splitting discreet intervals between high and low,
the Walsh and Menard preferred estimate hugs the low at the early
ages, then crosses to the high and even trespasses beyond it. The
behavior of the estimates is in reality a function of the distribution
of ages at which persons disappeared from the records; rather than
disappearing randomly they tended to drop from sight at particular
ages, 56 percent between 20 and 34 in this data set, 76 percent
before age 40. Nevertheless, to obtain a more aesthetic result, Walsh
and Menard added a refinement to their procedure, referring to it
briefly when, in closing their description of the method, they wrote
without elaboration: "In all of these calculations the unknowns

FIGURE 8

Years-Left-to-Live by Age Cohorts Derived Using
Walsh and Menard Method before and
after Refinement

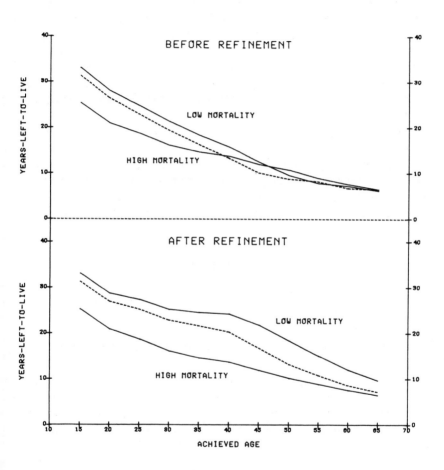

‖*Source and Note*: See text for derivation of the figure. Solid lines depict the
Walsh and Menard "High" and "Low" mortality estimates, the broken line their
"Preferred" estimate.

participated in the table through only the age cohort in which they last appear."[3] To understand this vastly important statement one must understand something of how a life table is put together.

Very simply, one accumulates from the data the number of persons who reach a specific age (call that age x and the accumulation of the number alive at age x l[x] or "little l at age x") together with the years lived by those persons between age x and the next age with which one is concerned (call this accumulation L[x] or "big L"). If, for example, we are going to be dealing with ages 20 and 25 and a person enters into the sample at exact age 20 to die at exact age 27, we would augment l[20] and l[25] by one to indicate his presence at these ages, augment L[20] by five to indicate he lived through his 20th, 21st, 22nd, 23rd, and 24th years, but only add two to L[25] inasmuch as he lived only the two years, ages 25 and 26. When all these accumulations are completed one cumulates the person–years-lived from the bottom to obtain for each age the total number of person–years-lived by all subjects after that age, or T[x]. The number of years of life expected to be lived upon achieving any particular age is simply the mean of the number of years actually lived after that age by the members of the sample:

$$T[x] \; / \; l[x]$$

To return to the Walsh and Menard phrase "in all these calculations the unknowns participated in the table through only the age cohort in which they last appear": If Walsh and Menard knew the age of death of one of their subjects, they allowed the accumulation to proceed normally. If, however, they had in hand one of the "unknowns" —a person, for example, known to be alive at age 20, last recorded alive at age 21, but dying at an unknown age—they would use an amended procedure. His age at death would be assigned according to one of their assumptions, let us say for the sake of the example, exact age 38. They would then augment their accumulations as in table 4. The person–years-lived by the unknowns (L[x]) are always counted but not his presence following his age at last entry in the records (l[x]). The unknowns are "participating through only the age cohort in which they last appear." The effects of this refinement are seen in the lower segment of figure 8. The high mortality values are as before, for recall that the high mortality assumption was that unknowns died the day after their last appearance in the records;

axiomatically they did not participate beyond the age cohort in which they last appeared even in the initial calculations. Low mortality and preferred values, however, are altered in such a way as to allow the latter to fall gracefully between low and high boundaries. The puzzling anomaly has been done away with.[4] But at what cost?

Recall the way life expectancy for any particular age is calculated—by dividing the total number of years lived by all subjects under observation after that age by the number of subjects achieving that age. In dealing with the unknowns, Walsh and Menard augmented the numerator of this division until the age of assumed death, but augmented the denominator only through the age at which the subject was last observed alive. The product—life expectancy at any given age —is inevitably distorted.

TABLE 4

Hypothetical Life Table Accumulations
by the Walsh and Menard Method

Age x	l[x]	L[x]
20	+1	+5
25	+0	+5
30	+0	+5
35	+0	+3

‖*Source*: Assumes an individual known to be alive at age 20, last reocrded alive at age 21, and assigned an age at death of 38.

Moreover, the additional refinement forced a procedural contradiction when Walsh and Menard turned to mortality per se. In demography, mortality between two achieved ages and life expectancy given an achieved age are part of a seamless web of calculations. The latter is computed, as we have seen, by

$$T[x] \ / \ l[x].$$

The former—specifically, the probability of dying between one age and the next, call it $q[x]$—is found by dividing the number alive at one age ($l[x]$) by the number alive at the previous age ($l[x-n]$), where n is the number of years intervening between the two ages), and subtracting the result from one:

$$1 \ - \ (l[x] \ / \ l[x-n]).$$

Or it can be arrived at indirectly by first calculating m[x]— "little m" —as the number of subjects dying between any given age and the next, divided by the number of person-years-lived between the ages, and then estimating q[x] by

$$(2 * (n * m[x])) / (2 + (n * m[x])).$$

Whichever calculation is used, however, the intent is to describe the same mortality experience that gave rise to the table of life expectancy.[5] The mortality figure for each age group (q[x]) can be used to construct a table of survivors, that is to say, a table of the estimated proportion of persons achieving one age who survive to achieve the next age. Here is where the seamless web of calculations is most apparent, for given a table of survivors and of life expectancies depicting a single mortality experience, one should be able to duplicate the latter from the former. Walsh and Menard appear to conform to this seamlessness. Life table values derived from their survivorship table neatly parallel their original life table values.[6] But when the same reciprocity is tested with the Middlesex data, the test fails. Using the entirety of the Walsh and Menard method we derive both a life table and the age-specific mortality figures (q[x]) underlying that table; using the latter we create a table of survivors and, from it, attempt to recalculate the original life table. The result—wide divergence between the two—is illustrated in figure 9.

That a test of the seamless web of demographic computations succeeds using the results published by Walsh and Menard and fails on replication points up the procedural contradiction in their work. In calculating their life tables, the unknowns—those in their sample for whom they had no fixed date of death—"participated. . . only through the age cohort in which they last appear." But to calculate a mortality schedule and derive a table of survivors they removed the restriction on the unknowns and included "all participants, whether or not we know their age at death."[7] In effect, they forced their tables of life expectancy and survivors to conform.

We do not denigrate the pioneering efforts of Walsh and Menard. Yet the flaws in their procedures force us to ask if there is any other way by which we can arrive at a best estimate of the true mortality schedule between low and high estimates. Up to a point, whatever scheme is devised ought to take into account what is known

FIGURE 9

Years-Left-to-Live by Age Cohorts Derived from Data Using
Complete Walsh and Menard Method and from
Table of Survivors

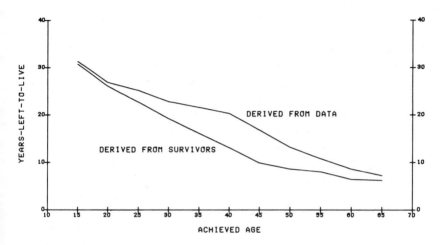

||*Source*: See text.

about the population in general and, specifically, of those disappearing
from the records. It must accept the possibility that disappearance
from the records might have been a function of the unrecorded
death of the subject. (Walsh and Menard's method does not allow
the possibility at all.)[8] Women whose last entry in the record
base is the birth of a child must surely be allowed at least the
possibility of dying in childbirth, while an immigrant servant, whose
single entry in the record is his arrival, must be accorded the
possibility of dying in the "seasoning" soon after. At the same time,
it must take into account the possibility that the disappearance was
simply a function of emigration from the county; the man (or woman)
simply moved on to live a full life elsewhere, dying in the aggregate
according to actuarial probabilities which presumably lie somewhere
between our high and low estimates.

We must keep in mind, too, that the nature of the records with
which we work is such that we are more likely to know that a man of

higher economic and social standing in the early Chesapeake was alive and well at any particular time than we are to know the same of a man of lower position. The higher–status man leaves his mark constantly—in being sworn into an office, serving on a jury, suing and being sued, buying and selling property, in his recorded commercial transactions. The lower–status man leaves his mark less frequently. Similarly, we are more likely to know of the death of a man of higher status than the death of a man of lower. The death of the former is registered more frequently; if it is unregistered, we are very likely to pick up his death from the probate of his will or the inventory of his estate. And his estate is more likely to be subject to suits at law. The death of a man of lower status is less likely to be registered. He is less likely to leave a will; his belongings are less likely to be inventoried. The lower the status, in other words, the easier it is for a man's death to become simply a disappearance. At the same time we must allow for a potential correlation between wealth and longevity as a function of differences in nutrition, clothing, and housing. The wealthier the man (or woman) the more likely he or she would be to eat well and be warm in winter. If the better sort suffered the gout to a greater exent than the lower orders, they were also less likely to die of pneumonia complicated by malnutrition. We cannot make too much of these correlations, obviously. Yet they hint to us that any group for whom we have a firm knowledge of death might be biased toward those of higher wealth and status who potentially lived longer, while the unknowns to whom we must assign an age at death might be biased toward those of lower wealth and status and potentially shorter lives. Whatever the scheme by which we assign ages of death to the unknowns, it must leave room for such potentials.

Until the advent of the Walsh and Menard method the accepted way to approximate the true mortality (and life expectancy) from the boundary estimates was simply to use the mean between extremes. Walsh and Menard offered no criticism of what they themselves termed "the usual practice."[9] But that usual practice seems intrinsically better than their own. The underlying assumption of the procedure is that given any group of 100 persons, all disappearing from the records at the same age—for the sake of example, exact age 20 and a low mortality estimate of years–left–to–live for persons achieving age 20 of 28—the ages of death of those disappearing would be normally distributed between 20 and 48. Some would die almost

immediately, encompassing the potential fate of women in childbirth
and immigrant servants. None would live beyond the age of 48, hence
the procedure effectively limits the possibility of those of lesser condition (a potential bias among the unknowns) achieving a greater
longevity than those of better condition (a potential bias among those
whose death we know). Most would die at or about the midpoint of
the range framed by our high and low mortality estimates.

In any event, this has been the procedure we have used to obtain
an initial estimate of mortality in Middlesex. We began by selecting a
group whose mortality experience was least affected by extraneous factors, a subset of the Middlesex population consisting of all
white, Chesapeake-born persons whose birth before 1730 we knew, and
who we knew lived to achieve at least the age of 15. The restriction
to the native born followed from our intention; we sought to gain, by
looking at mortality, a sense of the basic disease environment (including levels of nutrition, sanitation, and medical care) prevalent in the
society, hence excluded the immigrant who of necessity hazarded a
frequently fatal transition from one disease environment to another.
The restrictions as to age, date of birth, and race seemed necessary
in order to prevent the data from being overwhelmed by persons whose
date of death was unknown. The mortality experience of the sample—
821 males and 723 females, 1,544 individuals in all—is depicted in
figure 10.[10]

We stress that the figure represents an *initial* estimate, flawed
(or at least suspect) on two grounds, the first, of course, being
the underlying data. What demographers Ansley J. Coale and Paul
Demeny have written about modern data from large parts of the
world—"usually quite untrustworthy"—is true of most historical data,
no matter how carefully gathered or how scrupulously adjusted for
probable biases.[11] Our data are particularly suspect because of the
necessity of distributing so many unknowns. With one exception
(about which more later) the abrupt bulges and declivities in the
figure are more likely artifacts of the distribution than reflections
of reality. Secondly, the mortality schedules depicted are truncated.
The mortality experience of infants and children is not encompassed.
The simple fact of the matter is that data on age at death for those
dying under age 15 are so weak as to be virtually unusable.[12]
Infants undoubtedly appeared and disappeared, their lifespans
measured in days, without impressing either their birth or death on the
records from which we draw. And infants are recorded as born but

never appear in the records again. Any attempt to distribute their deaths across the age cohorts ends up little more than a matter of arbitrary assignment.

A resolution of both problems—untrustworthy data and infant and childhood mortality—seems to lie in an application to model life tables. Such tables are predicated upon the assumption that "persons of different ages in the same population share conditions that affect the health of all," hence clear, mathematical relationships exist between mortality expressions for different age groups.[13] Four "families" of such relationships have been isolated by demographers Coale and Demeny, and while the four do not exhaust all the possibilities by any means, they can constitute a standard for the moment. If we assume the absence of fatal hazards which significantly affected particular ages and not others, we can logically match our data to the most suitable family (or model) with the dual result of minimizing the result of bad data and extending the schedule to encompass missing age groups. Figure 11 shows such a match of our male data to the model best fitting them.[14] Translated into familiar terms, the figure indicates a society in which between four and five of every 10 new-born males died before their first birthday, while a male achieving age 20 could look forward to roughly 25 more years of life.

The extraordinarily high infant mortality—467 of every 1,000 new-born males failing to survive their first year—immediately engages our attention. The procedures used by Coale and Demeny have for some years been suspected of being flawed with respect to infant mortality in situations of high overall mortality, perhaps exaggerating young death by as much as 100 per 1,000.[15] We are obliged, therefore, to test the result.

Recall our sample of 821 native white males born prior to 1730 and known to have survived at least to age 15. Let us increase the sample to incorporate 682 males for whom we have a date of birth during these years but who cannot be demonstrated to have survived to their fifteenth birthdays. Our combined sample consists of 1,503 native born males. Only 62 of these are known to have died in infancy; 1,069 others are known to have survived their first year of life; the fate of 372 is unknown—they may have died that first year or they may have survived and died later. Let us assume momentarily that all died as infants, an improbable assumption but one which "stacks the deck" in favor of proving the high mortality arrived at by using Coale and Demeny. The assumed first year deaths, plus the 62 known, sum to

FIGURE 11

Best Fit of Model Life Table Mortality (q) to Initial Estimates
of Mortality among White Male Residents of Middlesex
Born in the Chesapeake Prior to 1730

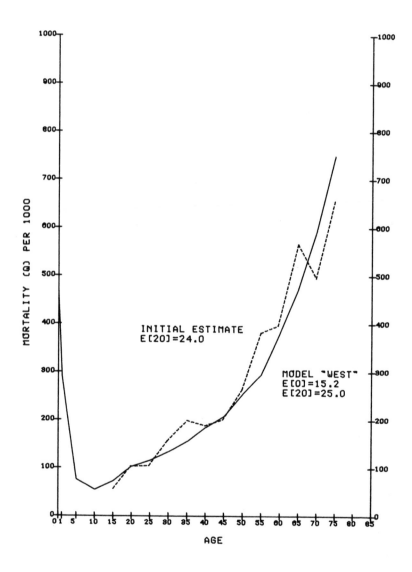

Source: See text.

434 or 28.9 percent of all births, a figure considerably shy of the percentage implied by fitting our data to a Coale and Demeny model.

We must go one step farther, however. What has been said before deserves saying again: No matter how much we know about births we know we do not know enough. How many instances were there of a birth and quick death, the infant leaving no mark at all on the historical record? Each such instance would, of course, drive our percentage of first year deaths upward.

To measure the impact of these unknown births and deaths we have recourse to data arranged for the purpose of studying fertility. Such data take the form of family reconstitutions, that is, linking a woman to her husband (or husbands) and children and establishing the age of the mother at each demographic event of her life and the intervals between events. Figure 12 is an example. By looking at virtually hundreds of populations demographers have established theoretical standards for childbearing within populations such as ours. A woman entering marriage will have a child within the first sixteen months or so and thereafter bear children roughly every 24 months, with the exact intervals varying according to the innate fecundity of the couple, the age of the woman and (to a lesser extent) her husband, the fate of a previous child, the length of time the woman breastfeeds her infant. Variations from this pattern—the appearance of gaps of 48 and 50 months or more between births—are indications of the incompleteness of the reconstitution, or, in the parlance of demographic historians, under-registration. In the figure, for example, the 38 months between the marriage of Elizabeth Sandeford and William Downing and the birth of William Downing, Jr., and the 47-month hiatus between Elizabeth and Thomas Chilton hint at missing children. By scanning a great many Middlesex reconstitutions looking for such gaps we can estimate the number of missed children. And by assuming that all the missing children died within a short time of birth—again unlikely as a matter of fact, still building the odds in favor of proving the Coale and Demeny procedure—then adding this number to the number of known and assumed infant deaths, we can obtain an outside estimate of infant mortality.

Positively, only 62 of the 1,503 native born males died in infancy, four out of every 100. When we assume that all those we do not know survived their first year actually died during its course (372), our percentage rises to 28.9. Scanning 831 Middlesex family reconstitutions encompassing 1,998 births indicates an error rate among

FIGURE 12

Illustrative Family Reconstitution from the
Middlesex Data Base

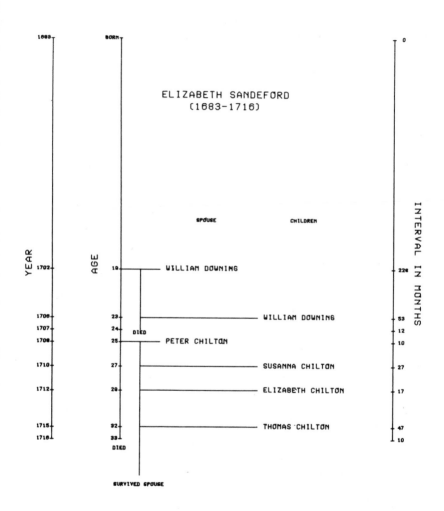

ELIZABETH SANDEFORD
(1683–1716)

males of 14.8 percent; that is, for every 100 known births there were in reality between 114 and 115.[16] The 1,503 known white male births, therefore, represent only a part of a more appropriate estimate of 1,727. Assuming all of the 222 missing births to have been infant deaths raises infant mortality among males to 38 percent, a considerable increase but still over eight points shy of the results obtained by utilizing the Coale and Demeny model—this despite the fact that in every instance we have biased our assumptions in favor of proving those results.

Clearly the mathematics of the Coale and Demeny model exaggerates infant mortality in situations such as ours. That exaggeration, however, does not preclude entirely our use of the model. There is no question but that it affords us an efficient and demographically sound way to smooth our "noisy" raw data. The exaggeration simply requires that mortality at the earlier ages be trimmed so as to fall within the boundary set by our outside estimate. The male segments of table 5 and figure 13 incorporate this trimming—the former our best estimate of the mortality experience of the native born males of Middlesex presented in the form of standard life table values.[17]

Unfortunately, the method of fitting our data to model life table values to arrive at a best estimate of mortality—the method utilized with male data—is not appropriate to data on females. Recall that the central assumption of model life tables is that "persons of different ages in the same population share conditions that affect the health of all"; in applying the model to males we assumed that no cause of death affected one age to any greater extent than any other age. We cannot make this assumption with regard to women for, as we have shown elsewhere, Middlesex was a highly malarious area and malaria, by its effect upon pregnant women, raises mortality among women in their childbearing years significantly.[18] Such a female "malarial bulge" is clearly evident in figure 10. As a consequence we have had to resort to another approach. We assume that the basic level of mortality is reflected by our best estimate of the male mortality schedule, hence start with its female complement, that is, the female mortality schedule mathematically associated with the level determined for the male. To this complementary female schedule we impart a malarial bulge by weighting mortality during the fertile years 15 through 49.[19] The female segment of table 5—our best estimate of female mortality—is the product of such a procedure. The general pattern, depicted in figure 13, seems accurate enough, but we stress

TABLE 5

Standardized Mortality Estimates for White Male and Female Residents
of Middlesex Born in the Chesapeake Prior to 1730

x	q	d	m	l	L	P	T	e
				M A L E S				
0	.356	356	.467	1000	762	.586	19690	19.7
1	.240	154	.071	644	2168	.808	18928	29.4
5	.067	33	.014	490	2367	.941	16761	34.2
10	.051	23	.010	457	2228	.939	14394	31.5
15	.072	31	.015	434	2091	.913	12166	28.0
20	.103	41	.022	402	1909	.891	10075	25.0
25	.115	42	.025	361	1701	.876	8166	22.6
30	.133	43	.029	319	1491	.857	6465	20.2
35	.155	43	.034	277	1277	.832	4974	18.0
40	.184	43	.041	234	1062	.805	3698	15.8
45	.208	40	.046	191	855	.772	2636	13.8
50	.254	38	.058	151	660	.728	1781	11.8
55	.295	33	.069	113	480	.669	1122	10.0
60	.382	30	.094	79	321	.583	641	8.1
65	.474	23	.124	49	187	.484	320	6.5
70	.595	15	.170	26	91	.360	133	5.2
75	.750	8	.240	10	33	.230	42	4.1
80	1.000	3	.268	3	10	.000	10	3.7
				F E M A L E S				
0	.308	308	.385	1000	800	.626	18658	18.7
1	.239	166	.071	692	2332	.811	17858	25.8
5	.072	38	.015	527	2539	.934	15526	29.5
10	.060	29	.012	489	2372	.917	12987	26.6
15	.107	49	.023	460	2176	.865	10616	23.1
20	.167	68	.036	411	1882	.827	8440	20.6
25	.181	62	.040	342	1556	.809	6558	19.2
30	.203	57	.045	280	1259	.790	5002	17.9
35	.220	49	.050	223	994	.776	3743	16.8
40	.228	40	.052	174	772	.769	2749	15.8
45	.233	31	.053	134	594	.783	1977	14.7
50	.195	20	.043	103	465	.784	1383	13.4
55	.241	20	.055	83	365	.716	918	11.1
60	.340	21	.082	63	261	.625	554	8.8
65	.427	18	.109	41	163	.522	293	7.1
70	.565	13	.158	24	85	.391	130	5.5
75	.709	7	.220	10	33	.252	45	4.3
80	1.000	3	.268	3	11	.000	11	3.7

that the numbers themselves are inferior in quality to those for males.

Thus far our findings apply only as a generalization of mortality in early Middlesex for we have aggregated data drawn from a broad period. We can, however, disaggregate the data, apply the same procedures, and gain a sense of change over time. Similarly, we can apply the procedures to those born elsewhere than in the Chesapeake, that is, to those immigrating into the region, and glimpse the effect upon lifespans of the exchange of the disease environment of old England for that of the Chesapeake. The results of such discreet analysis (table 6) tell a clear story.

Where the lifespans of immigrant and native-born males can be directly compared, the latter lived on average significantly longer than the former, a phenomenon also discerned by Walsh and Menard in their Maryland study. And through the last quarter of the seventeenth century the conditions determining mean age at death in Middlesex steadily deteriorated for both groups. Immigrants born prior to 1650, in all likelihood arriving in the Chesapeake in the late 1660s and 1670s, and achieving at least age 20 lived on average considerably longer (seven and more years) than those born in the 1650s and arriving in the late 1670s and early 1680s, while males born in the region in the 1670s and achieving age 20 had on average lifespans two and three years longer than their sons and grandsons. These table values emerge from the data as something of a surprise inasmuch as Chesapeake scholars have been assuming (although in the absence of firm evidence) that the fearful mortality of the seventeenth century miti-

---

‖*Source and Notes:* x = achieved age, q = probability at age x of dying before age x + n (where n is 1 between ages 0 and 1, 4 between ages 1 and 5, and elsewhere 5), d = number of deaths between ages x and x + n out of a hypothetical cohort of 1,000, m = death rate in the life table population (number of deaths per person-years-lived) between ages x and x + n, l = number of survivors at age x out of the original cohort, L = number of person-years-lived between ages x and x + n, P = proportion of persons in a given five-year age group alive five years later, with P[0] representing P[BIRTH], P[1] representing P[0,4], and P[75] computed by T[80] / T[75], T = person-years-lived at age x and over by the original cohort, and e = the average number of years remaining to be lived (expectation of life) upon achieving age x. The table was derived from a fitting of initial estimates of m[15,80], male, to the m schedule of the most appropriate model and level (viz., Model West, Male, Index e[10] = 17.1104) using the mathematics of Ansley J. Coale and Paul Demeny, *Regional Model Life Tables and Stable Populations* (Princeton, 1966), 20–29, adjusting male and female infant and childhood mortality and female mortality 15–49 as described in the text.

FIGURE 13

Best Estimates of Age-Specific Mortality (q) among White Male
and Female Residents of Middlesex Born in the Chesapeake
Prior to 1730

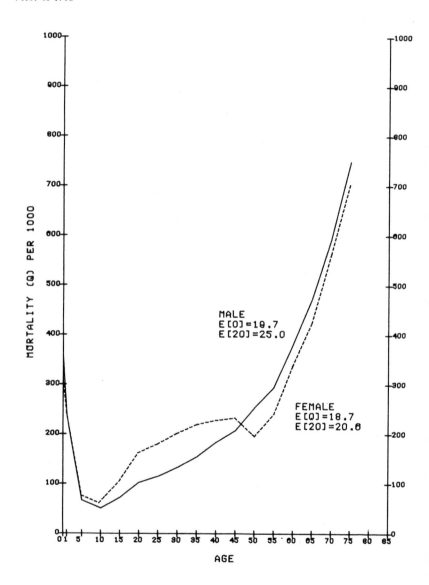

TABLE 6

Mortality Estimates by Time for Immigrant and
Chesapeake-Born Male Residents of
Middlesex Achieving Age 20

Born in Decade	Would Be 20-24 between	*N*	Mortality 20-24 per 100 (q)	Expected Years to Live at Age 20
IMMIGRANT				
1630-1649	1650-1674	71	5.6	34.0
1650-1659	1670-1684	100	8.1	28.6
1660-1669	1680-1694	125	13.5	21.0
1670-1679	1690-1704	43	13.2	21.3
CHESAPEAKE-BORN				
1670-1679	1690-1704	61	9.4	26.4
1680-1689	1700-1714	117	10.9	24.1
1690-1699	1710-1724	125	11.4	23.5
1700-1709	1720-1734	143	11.0	24.1
1710-1719	1730-1744	135	11.2	23.8
1720-1729	1740-1754	109	11.3	23.6

‖*Source*: See text.

gated in the eighteenth as the native born came to predominate in the population.[20] At least in Middlesex, wracked as it was by devasting epidemics in the later century, this was not the case.

A caveat to all these numbers is in order. Incomplete and biased data and the necessity of applying correctives makes historical demography generally a far from exact art, hence the numbers reported here should be accepted for their broad suggestions rather than as precise values. And even the broad suggestions are to be drawn by comparisons. Demographic numbers have limited intrinsic meaning. They gain meaning only in relationship to numbers similarly calculated from other populations. Thus an e[20] for males of roughly 25 years—a man reaching age 20 had on the average 25 years of life left—means something largely in terms of a modern e[20] of roughly twice that, or an e[20] from seventeenth-century England of roughly 32, or an e[20] drawn from Maryland data (but computed differently) of 26.[21] Comparison with the last—and with results from other areas of the Chesapeake—indicates that in terms of mortality Middlesex was roughly representative of the whole region. The other comparisons show that the mortality experience of the Chesapeake and the conditions of disease, nutrition, and sanitation which underlay it were alien both in their own time and in terms of ours. Indeed, the model life tables to which we have referred were designed to encompass the entire range of modern mortality from both undeveloped and developed nations; mortality in the early Chesapeake quite literally drops off these published tables.[22]

|●|

1. Lorena S. Walsh and Russell R. Menard, "Death in the Chesapeake: Two Life Tables for Men in Early Colonial Maryland," *Maryland Historical Magazine*, LXIX (1974), 211–227. Although consciously working in the tradition of French demographic historians, Walsh and Menard used a method utilized by American scholars at least as early 1958. See Sidney J. Cutler and Fred Ederer, "Maximum Utilization of the Life Table Method in Analyzing Survival," *Journal of Chronic Diseases*, VIII (1958), 699-712.

2. "Originally when we cranked through the knowns and unknowns in the conventional manner (not removing the unknowns at age of last appearance) we ran into problems. . . [which] made the table look puzzling." Walsh to the authors, April 25, 1979.

3. Walsh and Menard, "Death in the Chesapeake," *Md. Hist. Mag.*, LXIX (1974), 213.

4. In response to a description of our Fortran routine operationalizing their method as described here, Menard wrote: "Yes, I think your procedure replicates our method exactly." Walsh responded by illustrating the preferred estimate: "Suppose a native man was present from birth and disappeared at age 31. To establish the preferred estimate we would add the life expectancy established for the knowns (31 +17.6 = 48.6). His presence is counted at achieved ages of 20, 25, and 30. His person years lived are then added in also only at 20, 25, and 30 (to keep numerator and denominator balanced). Subsequently he is totally removed from the calculations." Such a procedure, however, would enter into the calculations the death of the unknown at age 31 and the preferred estimate would correspond to the high mortality estimate. Menard to the authors, April 11, 1979, Walsh to the authors, April 25, 1979.

5. George W. Barclay, *Techniques of Population Analysis* (New York, 1958), 108, 114–115.

6. The table of survivors for native males in Walsh and Menard, "Death in the Chesapeake," *Md. Hist. Mag.*, LXIX (1974), 217 produces the following life expectancies (the "preferred estimate" which they derived directly from data is in parentheses): at age 20, 26.5 (26.0), age 30, 20.8 (20.4), age 40, 15.2 (15.6), age 50, 11.7 (12.0), age 60, 8.1 (9.3), age 70, 5.0 (7.0). The congruence can only be approximate when using intervals between ages greater than 1 for in reconstructing life expectancies from tables of survivors all deaths are presumed to

take place at the cohort mid-points.

7. Walsh and Menard, "Death in the Chesapeake," *Md. Hist. Mag.*, LXIX (1974), 216.

8. The unknowns are always assumed to die subsequent to their disappearance, viz., at the age of disappearance plus the years left to live derived from the known deaths alone. In the Middlesex data used to replicate the Walsh and Menard procedure, 94 of the 121 unknowns disappeared before the age of 40 yet none of the 121 was assigned an age at death of less than 45.

9. Walsh and Menard, "Death in the Chesapeake," *Md. Hist. Mag.*, LXIX (1974), 213.

10. An exact date of death has been established for 520 males (63.3%) and 338 females (46.7%).

11. Ansley J. Coale and Paul Demeny, *Regional Model Life Tables and Stable Populations* (Princeton, N.J., 1966), 29.

12. An additional 1,370 births are known, all individuals who are not known to have achieved age 15; of these only 366 (26.7%) have a known death date. The necessity of distributing 73.3% of the sample vitiates its use.

13. Ansley J. Coale, *The Growth and Structure of Human Populations: A Mathematical Investigation* (Princeton, N.J., 1972), 9.

14. Our procedure has been to compute m[x=15,80] from the data by the method described in the text and compare the series to model life table values of m successively computed—following Coale and Demeny, *Regional Model Life Tables*, 20-26— from the appropriate Index e[10] plus and minus an iteration factor of 0.01. Each of the four "families" was tested in turn and the best fit selected by a least-squares test. In effect the procedure—obviously impossible without recourse to a computer— allowed us to establish both the best fitting family and best fitting extrapolation from Level 1 of that family. We used m values rather than q values to establish the fit because the nature of the original data did not allow a direct calculation of the latter; we could only approximate q from the data by the indirect method described in the text. The best fit was obtained with model West using an Index e[10] of 17.1104 and resulted in an e[0] of 15.2 and e[20] of 25.0.

15. Jack E. Eblen, "New Estimates of the Vital Rates of the United States Black Population during the Nineteenth Century," *Demography*, XI (1974), 302. Eblen argues for an alternative strategy developed in United Nations, Department of Economic and Social Affairs, *The Concept of a Stable Population: Applications to the Study of Populations of Countries with Incomplete Demographic Statistics* (New York, 1968), 99-115. This strategy, however, has only marginal utility in very high mortality situations (p. 153), indeed, it is not even applied below U.N. Level 20, while the Middlesex data suggests the appropriateness of a level below Level 0.

16. See below under "Fertility," for a description of the sample and the procedure used to estimate missing births. The overall error rate was 14.2% with a correction factor of 1.166—1,000 known births implying 1,166 true births, hence 166 missing births per 1,000. The necessity of converting this overall error rate to a male error rate follows from an empirical sex ratio at birth of 108 males per 100 females, a small but significant departure from a normal 105. Logically, we

are more likely to lose a female birth than a male. Unregistered at birth yet surviving to maturity, the male had many more opportunities to impress his age and parentage on the historical record—in a deposition, for example, or a conveyance citing land patented by his father—than had his female counterpart. The sex ratio at birth seems to confirm the logic. We convert the overall error rate to a male error rate by assuming a sex distribution among the missing children such as to lead to a normal sex ratio. The following illustrates on the basis of 1,000 known births:

	Total Births	Male	Female	Sex Ratio
Known	1,000	520	480	108
x	1.166	1.148	1.185	
Estimate	1,166	597	569	105

17. We assumed that those disappearing between birth and exact age 15 died in the same proportion as did those whose age at death can be ascertained, hence set 35.6% as a maximum for deaths between age 0 and 1.

18. Darrett B. and Anita H. Rutman, "Of Agues and Fevers: Malaria in the Early Chesapeake," *WMQ*, 3d Ser., XXXIII (1976), 31–60. Attempts to fit our female data to female models produced intuitively ludicrous results and, of course, wiped out the malarial bulge.

19. The weights by which complementary female q values 15–49 were multiplied were computed from data in Samuel H. Preston, et al., *Causes of Death: Life Tables for National Populations* (New York, 1972), 702–703, viz.,

$$W[x] = (qT[x] / q[x]) + ((qT[x] / 2) / (q[x] / 2))$$

where $W[x]$ is the weight at age x, $qT[x]$ represents the mortality schedule for Taiwanese women, 1920, all causes of death combined, and $q[x]$ the mortality schedule for the same women with maternal deaths eliminated. The weight for women 15–19 was adjusted downward to compensate for the smaller proportion of the age group married in Middlesex. For the rationale for the use of such tables see Preston, *Mortality Patterns in National Populations With Special Reference to Recorded Causes of Death* (New York, 1976), passim and his earlier article, "Influence of Cause of Death Structure on Age Patterns of Mortality," in T. N. E. Greville, *Population Dynamics* (New York, 1972), 201–250. It is impossible to make a direct adjustment for malaria inasmuch as the fatal effects of the disease are generally subsumed under various other causes of death. See Rutman and Rutman, "Of Agues and Fevers," *WMQ*, 3d Ser., XXXIII (1976), 50.

20. Walsh and Menard, "Death in the Chesapeake," *Md. Hist. Mag.*, LXIX (1974), 213, Allan Kulikoff, "The Colonial Chesapeake: Seedbed of Antebellum Southern Culture?" *Journal of Southern History*, XLV (1979), 533; Lorena S. Walsh, "'Till Death Us Do Part': Marriage and Family in Seventeenth-Century Maryland," in Thad W. Tate and David L. Ammerman, eds., *The Chesapeake in the Seventeenth Century: Essays in Anglo-American Society* (Chapel Hill, N.C., 1979, 150–151. The life tables generated by James M. Gallman, "Mortality among Males: Colonial North Carolina," *Social Science History*, IV (1980), 300 suggest, as we do, a rising rather than declining mortality.

21. In addition to the life tables generated by Walsh and Menard, "Death in the Chesapeake," *Md. Hist. Mag.*, LXIX (1974), 213, 214 and Gallman, "Mortality among White Males," *Soc. Sci. Hist.*, IV (1980), 300, see Daniel Blake Smith, "Mortality and Family in the Colonial Chesapeake," *Journ. Int. Hist.*, VIII (1978), 403–427, and Darrett B. and Anita H. Rutman, "'Now-Wives and Sons-in-Law': Parental Death in a Seventeenth-Century Virginia County," in Tate and Ammerman, eds., *Chesapeake in the Seventeenth Century*, 177–182. The figures in all of these, together with those reported in table 5, indicate a significant departure from both New England and English levels. On the latter see e.g., Lawrence Stone, *The Family, Sex and Marriage in England 1500-1800* (New York, 1977), 71; E. A. Wrigley, "Mortality in Pre-Industrial England: The Example of Colyton, Devon, Over Three Centuries," *Daedalus* (Spring, 1968), 561. The survivorship tables in Wrigley convert to an e[25] for males and females combined born 1625–1699 and 1700–1774 of 29.9 and 34.3.

22. The lowest mortality level generally calculated for model tables is based upon a female e[0] of 20 years; the lowest male mortality level in the published tables in Coale and Demeny, *Regional Model Life Tables* offers an e[0] of 17.5.

five

FERTILITY

Fertility—more appropriately, but not customarily, called natality—is the measurement of the number of live births in a population and speaks ultimately to questions of family size and the ability of a population to reproduce itself and grow by natural means. Such things will vary in concert with cultural and natural factors. The fertile years of a woman are biologically limited in number, usually considered to be those lived from ages 15 through 44 inclusively, or 15 through 49. But her childbearing is dependent upon access to the male which in turn is dependent upon the culture. If in one culture legitimate access (marriage) does not occur until the woman is on the average 18 while in a second access does not occur until 25, the total fertility of the latter culture will be lower than that of the former. If a culture practices conscious family limitation, the number of live births will obviously be fewer than in one that does not. Mortality, the age structure of the population, divorce and separations which end marriages prematurely, all play roles. If, in a particular situation, death tends to strike down women in their late 30s or a high rate of mid-life divorce separates many women permanently from husbands, the society will not have the children

that might have been born to the women in their 40s. Similarly,
the death of husbands and the rate at which widows remarry affect
fertility by removing women from the risk of pregnancy and childbirth, at least for a while.

Add to such complexities the complexity of data. We have
already (in our section on "Mortality") referred to the fact that
what we know of births derives from ordering data on marriages and
births to "reconstitute" the families of 831 Middlesex women whose
birth dates prior to 1735 we knew and whose children's births (if
any) could be dated. The reconstitutions, however, give us only a
minimal knowledge of births. We must assume that an unknown number of additional children escaped the record-keeping process upon
which we depend and attempt to compensate for the error. Our way
has been to scan the reconstitutions for improbably long intervals
between births and, on the basis of the number of such, estimate
the number of missing children. Specifically, we have for each
reconstitution computed the average interval and statistical
variance; where the variance has exceeded 150—a standard set by
demographers—we have assumed a missing birth in the largest interval, split that interval in half and recomputed the average and
variance, continuing the process (and asuming additional missing
children) until the variance fell below the 150 mark. The estimate
of missing births becomes, as we shall see, the basis for computing
an error factor by which we convert empirical fertility measures to
approximations of the true measures.[1]

Add, finally, complexities associated with the measurement of
fertility itself. The very way in which we count births will have
us measuring quite different, albeit related, phenomena. Thus we
can count births occurring to all women during specific years to
measure time-specific or "calendar" fertility, or count all births
to a select group of women born at a particular time and measure
"cohort" fertility. When fertility is not changing over time the
two measurements will produce the same result. As we shall see,
however, fertility in Middlesex did change over time as defining
variables changed.

One cultural facet of the problem of fertility we can immediately dismiss. There is no evidence of conscious family limitation
in Middlesex in our period. Indeed, there is positive evidence of
its absence. When legitimate births to married Middlesex women
surviving and under observation throughout their childbearing years

are converted to age-specific fertility rates—that is, the number of births per 100 years lived by the women at particular ages—and the values are plotted on a graph, the resulting curve displays the familiar convexity of what is termed natural fertility rather than the concavity associated with deliberate birth control. Figure 14 illustrates the test, depicting the Middlesex curve and a natural fertility curve projected by the French demographer Louis Henry as

FIGURE 14

Natural Fertility and the Fertility of Married Middlesex
Women Born through 1729 and under Observation
throughout Their Childbearing Years

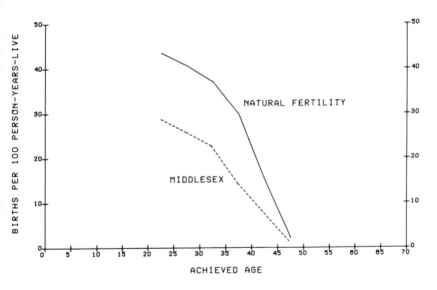

|Source and Notes: The natural fertility curve is from Louis Henry,"Some Data on Natural Fertility," *Eugenics Quarterly*, VIII (1961), 81-91; the Middlesex curve is derived from data on 114 married women drawn from the Middlesex biographies described in chapter 1 who were under observation throughout their childbearing years 15-49. Unadjusted birth data were utilized in computing fertility as (B / PYL) * 100 where B is the number of births occurring to the women at each particular age (20-24, 25-29. . . 45-49) and PYL is the number of years lived by them at those ages. Completed family size for the women (unadjusted) computes to 5.7. See note 2 for Coale's "m," a summary measure of departure from natural fertility.

a mean for populations unmarked by conscious family limitation. Fertility in Middlesex is obviously under this mean curve, but for now the configuration alone is the point at issue. It is roughly the same.[2]

We can, moreover, bring a number of relevant elements into immediate purview. Mortality has been discussed earlier. In table 7 we present the mean age at first marriage for 1,478 Middlesex residents grouped by the date of the marriage and our knowledge as to whether or not an individual had at any time been a servant. The age at which men first married is not, of course, directly perti-

TABLE 7

Age at First Marriage for Male and Female Residents of Middlesex, 1650–1750, by Year of Marriage

Married	Male				Female			
	N	Md	Mn	SD	*N*	Md	Mn	SD
FORMER SERVANTS								
1670–1689	14	27.0	27.4	4.2	*	*	*	*
1680–1689	27	26.2	27.3	3.6	18	22.6	22.9	2.4
1690–1699	24	28.1	29.0	4.4	5	19.6	20.5	2.0
1700–1709	31	27.0	30.0	6.8	6	20.3	21.3	2.3
1710–1719	17	27.3	28.9	5.5	*	*	*	*
ALL OTHERS								
Thru 1669	17	28.2	30.8	8.9	19	18.0	19.6	5.6
1670–1679	14	25.0	27.1	5.6	23	17.0	18.1	3.4
1680–1689	45	24.1	25.8	5.4	59	17.0	17.5	2.6
1690–1699	44	25.0	26.6	6.1	47	18.0	17.9	3.5
1700–1709	89	24.0	25.0	4.9	103	18.7	19.6	3.7
1710–1719	89	23.3	25.1	4.6	85	19.5	20.1	4.5
1720–1729	96	24.5	25.1	4.8	110	19.7	20.3	3.7
1730–1739	115	23.1	24.1	4.1	121	20.5	20.8	3.6
1740–1749	131	26.4	27.5	6.4	110	21.3	22.0	4.3

‖*Source and Note:* The table is based upon the Middlesex biographies described in chapter 1. An asterisk (*) indicates a number of cases insufficient for computation. Here and elsewhere in the tables that follow the abbreviations Mn (Mean), Md (Median), and SD (Standard Deviation) are used.

TABLE 8

Age at First Marriage for Male and Female Residents of
Middlesex, 1650-1750, by Year of Birth

Born	Male				Females			
	N	Md	Mn	SD	*N*	Md	Mn	SD
FORMER SERVANTS								
Thru 1669	70	28.0	29.5	5.5	21	22.6	22.8	2.3
1670-1679	21	26.9	28.9	5.2	6	19.7	23.9	8.6
1680-1689	22	25.7	27.2	6.3	8	20.6	22.9	4.0
ALL OTHERS								
Thru 1669	105	26.9	28.4	6.8	86	17.8	18.7	4.0
1670-1679	53	25.0	26.7	5.3	59	17.5	18.8	5.0
1680-1689	92	24.0	25.2	5.1	97	19.5	20.3	4.2
1690-1699	90	23.0	24.7	4.6	94	19.1	19.6	3.8
1700-1709	108	24.3	25.0	4.3	118	20.0	20.6	4.2
1710-1719	109	23.0	24.4	4.5	119	20.2	20.5	3.4
1720-1729	48	23.8	25.0	5.1	53	20.4	20.9	3.5
1730-1739	27	27.9	28.9	7.4	32	20.8	21.3	4.0

‖*Source:* See table 7. 1740-1749 "All Others" is omitted as having
too few data points for meaningful computations.

nent to fertility but we have included male data in the interest of
a complete presentation. Table 8 presents the same data regrouped
by date of birth of the subject (the wife in forming the female
table, the husband in forming the male table).[3]

Keep in mind when considering these tables that our knowledge
of former servitude is always incomplete. Some men and women undoubtedly entered the county as servants, labored for a number of
years, but left their first mark in the records only after achieving
their freedom. In such instances we would be ignorant of their
past servitude and they would be tabulated under "All Others"
rather than "Former Servants." The first few categories of the
former—the bottom segment of each table—would seem, therefore,
overestimates when "All Others" is construed as "Never a Servant."
But the extent of the error steadily diminishes through the chrono-
logical categories of the tables inasmuch as the number of servants
declined over time and the number of native-born sons and daughters

maturing and marrying rose. We will not be far off the mark if, in conceptualizing "All Others" as "Never a Servant" in table 7, we mentally reduce the age of women marrying for the first time in the years through 1689 to between 16 and 17 and to between 17 and 18 for the years 1690-1699. (In the same way we will not be far off if we reduce mentally the male age at first marriage for "All Others" through these years.)[4]

With this adjustment in mind, and ignoring the fluctuations of age at marriage for female servants—insignificant in view of the small numbers involved—two things become clear. First, servitude delayed the marriage of women by as much as five and six years. Second, the mean age at first marriage for those who did not spend years in servitude (largely the native born daughters and grand-daughters of the first settlers) was steadily rising over time, from between 16 and 17 in the years before 1670, to 19 and 20 in the first decade of the eighteenth century, and reaching 21 and 22 at the end of the period. Obviously servitude tended to remove women from the pool of potential mothers for a number of years, but inasmuch as white servitude was steadily diminishing, the dampening effect of this on any fertility measure would diminish and fertility would steadily rise.[5] At the same time, however, a rising age at first marriage for an enlarging body of native born would have just the opposite effect.

TABLE 9

Remarriage in Middlesex by Date of End of
Marriage, 1650-1750

Marriage Ended	N	Surviving		Remarrying		Interval in Years			
		Husb	Wife	Husb	Wife	Husb		Wife	
		(%)		(%)		Mn	SD	Mn	SD
Thru 1689	314	57.0	43.0	38.5	69.6	2.8	4.9	2.5	4.4
1690-1709	358	54.7	45.3	41.8	59.3	2.0	3.2	2.2	3.8
1710-1749	731	52.9	47.1	39.8	43.6	1.7	2.2	2.2	2.9
Thru 1749	1403	54.3	45.7	40.0	53.0	2.0	3.3	2.3	3.6

||*Source and Note:* The table is derived from the Middlesex biographies des-
cribed in chapter 1. In every category the median interval to remarriage was
one year.

TABLE 10

Percentage Remarrying in Middlesex by Date and Age of
Survivor at End of Prior Marriage, 1650-1750

Marriage Ended	N	Age of Survivor						All
		-20	20-29	30-39	40-49	50-59	60+	
		SURVIVING HUSBAND						
Thru 1689	88	**	62.2 4.0	82.9 2.4	66.7* 3.0*	66.7* 0.3*	0.0*	70.5 3.0
1690-1709	108	0.0*	60.0 2.1	81.4 1.8	65.0 2.2	100.0* 0.8*	**	70.4 1.9
1710-1749	212	50.0* 6.4*	71.4 1.6	73.6 1.9	71.1 1.7	72.2 0.9	50.0* 1.0*	71.7 1.9
Thru 1749	408	33.0 6.4*	65.7 2.3	76.6 2.0	68.6 2.1	76.0 0.8	40.0* 0.9*	71.1 2.0
		SURVIVING WIFE						
Thru 1689	92	100.0 3.3	90.2 3.1	81.8 1.7	85.7* 1.3*	0.0*	**	89.1 2.7
1690-1709	109	92.0 3.6	90.6 2.0	71.4 1.9	85.7* 0.3*	0.0*	0.0*	84.4 2.3
1710-1749	200	79.2 1.9	87.2 2.5	69.5 2.1	76.0 1.5	27.3 1.8*	0.0*	75.0 2.2
Thru 1749	401	90.0 3.0	89.5 2.5	72.6 1.9	79.5 1.2	21.4 1.8*	0.0*	80.8 2.3

‖*Source and Notes:* The table is derived from the Middlesex biographies
described in chapter 1. Only survivors remaining in observation at least 10 years
following the end of a marriage are included. Mean intervals to remarriage are
entered below the percentage of survivors remarrying. An asterisk (*) indicates
fewer than 10 cases, a double asterisk (**) no cases.

Marriage in Middlesex was for life. Divorce and separation
were all but unknown. But life was, as we have seen, relatively
short. Widows and widowers were very much a part of the scene.
Tables 9 and 10 present data based upon 1,403 marriages from the
years through 1749 for which we can determine the surviving
partners. Just under half of these marriages ended with the wife

surviving; 91.4 percent of the widows were still in their childbearing years.[6] In one respect—the percent of survivors remarrying—the first of these tables is misleading. Incorporated into the sample are those survivors who died or departed the county soon after the dissolution of the marriage. They were, consequently, not "at risk" to remarry and their inclusion in the tabulation creates erroneously low remarriage percentages. The second table confines the sample to those remaining under observation for at least ten years following the end of the marriage. In it, too, we have broken down

FIGURE 15

Female Mortality, Age at First Marriage, and Percent
of Widows Remarrying in Middlesex, 1650–1750

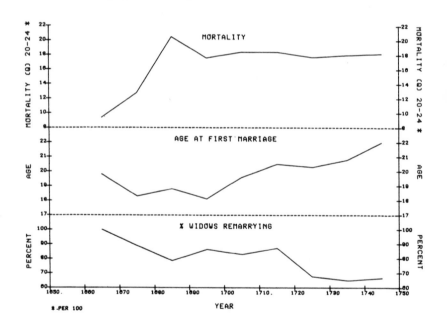

‖*Source and Notes*: Female mortality (q) at age 20–24, derived by the procedure outlined under under "Mortality," exemplifies the general level of health. Decadal estimates of age at first marriage and percentage of widows remarrying are disaggregations of data from tables 7 and 10 with the first two decades combined because of small sample sizes. Data are plotted on the midpoints of decades.

remarriage by the age of the surviving partner at the end of the
dissolved marriage and entered the mean interval between the end
of one marriage and the entrance into the next. Although the latter
varied somewhat with the age of the widow, the overall constancy
across time is remarkable. But for the purpose of analyzing fertility the important element of this second table is the slight
decline over time in the percentage of widows remarrying, a decline
that, like the rising age at first marriage, would tend to dampen
overall fertility. The decline shows up even more clearly in
figure 15, a decadal breakdown of the three factors which most
affect fertility—female mortality (expressed in terms of the probability of achieving age 25 having reached age 20 as derived by the
method described in the last section), age at first marriage, and
the percent of widows remarrying.

When we turn to fertility per se we are fortunate in that our
family reconstitutions allow us to group and measure both calendar
and cohort fertility with one sequence of operations. The reconstitutions, recall, link the women, their husbands, and their children
in succession according to the age of the woman at each event. The
births are extracted from the reconstitutions and aggregated according to both the date of birth of the mother and her age at the
time of the birth. The aggregate counts themselves are arranged in
matrix form, together with counts of the number of years lived in
marriage by the women at particular ages. Births divided by the
years-lived-married, the product adjusted to account for both the
proportion of the women of the cohort married at the given age and
the number of children presumed missing from the reconstitutions,
then multiplied by the number of years encompassed by the age
category, provides for each cell of the matrix a fertility measure
applicable to the women at that age—specifically, the average number of children born to women of the cohort during the years of life
involved. This tedious but not particularly complex series of operations can be illustrated in terms of the marked cell in figure 16:

Number of women born 1690-1694
achieving age 20   61

Number of these living in marriage
at any time age 20 through 24   47

Legitimate births to women born 1690–1694 at age 20–24	54
Total number of years lived in marriage by these women at age 20–24	170
Age–specific marital birth rate (54 / 170)	0.318
Proportion of the women married at any time 20–24 (47 / 61)	0.770
Age–specific birth rate (0.770 * 0.318)	0.245
Error factor: Number of births assumed missed in the reconstitutions of women born 1690–1694 (16), plus all known births to these women (222), the sum divided by all births to the women (222)	1.131
Adjusted age–specific birth rate (1.131 * 0.245)	0.277
Average number of children born to women themselves born 1690–1694 at age 20–24 (0.277 * 5)	1.39

We need only sum down or diagonally through the matrix of final values to establish summary calendar and cohort indices of fertility, as the partial matrix depicted in figure 16 illustrates.

Consider the vertical column on the left, devoted to women born 1690 through 1694. Reading down we have age–specific fertility rates for these women, the sum of which constitutes the *average number of children ever born to*, or *average completed family of*, the women of the cohort. Now consider the diagonal, starting with the upper right. That cell carries an age–specific rate reflecting births

FIGURE 16

The Computation of Calendar and Cohort Fertility

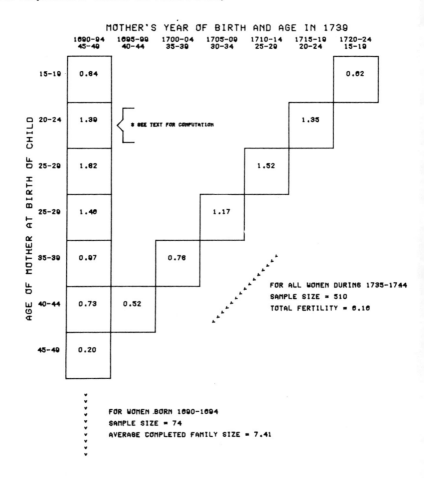

MOTHER'S YEAR OF BIRTH AND AGE IN 1739

FOR ALL WOMEN DURING 1735-1744
SAMPLE SIZE = 510
TOTAL FERTILITY = 8.10

FOR WOMEN BORN 1690-1694
SAMPLE SIZE = 74
AVERAGE COMPLETED FAMILY SIZE = 7.41

||*Source:* See text.

to women born 1720–1724 during their 15th through 19th years of age. But note that women born 1720–1724 would be passing through the age category 15–19 during the years 1735–1744. In those same years our women born 1690–1694 would be passing through the age category 45–49 (the cell at the other end of the diagonal). Similarly, women born 1695–1699 would be passing through their 40th through 44th years. And so on all along the diagonal. Summing the diagonal, there—

fore, gives us a *total fertility rate*, or what the average number of children ever born to women 15–49 would have amounted to *if* the conditions underlying fertility had never varied from the conditions during the calendar period in question—in this case 1735–1744.[7] The two rates are easily confused but they refer to quite different things. Average completed family size derives from (and applies to) the concept of a single group of women observed throughout their fertile years, their fertility the result of ever changing conditions. The total fertility rate derives from a group of women of varying ages, all subject to (and reflecting in the fertility measure) essentially one set of time-specific conditions.

TABLE 11

Crude Birth Rates for Middlesex
for Select Years

Year	Births Per 1000 Population
1668	24.7
1687	40.9
1699	31.3
1704	36.0
1724	47.2
1740	48.2

||*Source:* Derived by the procedure described in Darrett B. and Anita H. Rutman, "'More True and Perfect Lists:' The Reconstruction of Censuses for Middlesex County, Virginia, 1668–1704," *Virginia Magazine of History and Biography*, CLXXVIII (1980), 65–66. The slight variation from values reported earlier follows from a refinement of the reconstructed census of 1668.

Average completed family size and total fertility are by no means the easiest fertility statistics to compute or comprehend. Other rates are far simpler, the crude birth rate, for example—so many births per 1,000 population. But such simpler rates are extraordinarily sensitive to factors extraneous to what we want to measure. For comparative purposes we offer in table 11 crude birth rates for the years for which we have reconstructed censuses. The table, however, speaks more to the changing nature of the population than it does to the childbearing of its women, the low rate for 1668 following from the presence of a large servant body, predominantly male and forbidden by law from procreating. The rates depicted in figure 17 are free of such "noise," for being computed solely on the basis of the women of childbearing age they reflect only those things which truly affect fertility.[8]

FIGURE 17

Average Completed Family Size and Total Fertility
by Time in Middlesex, 1650-1750

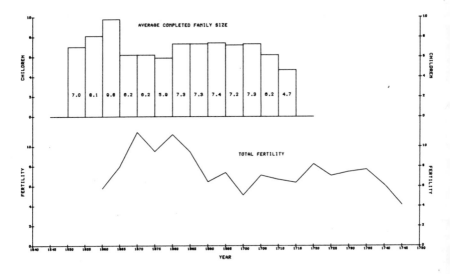

||*Source*: See text.

The bar graph at the top of the figure represents the average completed family size of women born in the five-year cohorts 1650–1654, 1655–1659. . . 1710–1714, assuming that the women lived through their childbearing years. The experiences represented by these numbers are the product of conditions prevailing during the years stretching forward from the women's birth years, summed up in the total fertility statistics depicted by the line graph in the figure. There is obviously random chatter emanating from faulty data operating on the latter. Yet even taking this into account it seems clear enough that something radical is happening to fertility in the county. Rising nicely as the age of first marriage drops (recall figure 15), fertility plateaus at around 11, then drops abruptly to establish a constant at between 6.5 and 7.5 until, at the end of the period, a rising age at first marriage and declining percentage of widows remarrying pushes it down again. The obvious question is why the abrupt decline in the late 1680s? The answer seems to lie

79

in the similarity between the mortality curve in figure 15 and the
total fertility curve depicted here.

To understand the interrelationship of the two curves we must
realize first that such fertility statistics as we are using are
generally considered to be free of the effects of mortality. The
numbers are computed solely on the basis of births to living women,
viz:

$$B[x] \, / \, PYL[x]$$

where B represents the number of births to women of age x and PYL
the number of years lived by women at that age. If mortality rises
(as it did in the 1680s) and women die at a greater rate, that fact
cannot directly affect our measurement of fertility; the women will
simply not be on hand to contribute either births or person years
to the computation. If, however, the conditions underlying the rise
in mortality are of a particular kind, those same conditions will
affect the measurement of fertility as well. The particularities of
falciparum malaria—an African form of the disease previously
unknown to Englishmen and women which, we have argued elsewhere,
entered the Chesapeake in the 1680s—establish just such conditions.[9]
Far more virulent and devastating than the *vivax* malaria which came
with the settlers from England, the new malaria was particularly
hard on pregnant women, inducing fetal deaths and abortions,
stillbirths, and childbed deaths of both mothers and infants. All of
these would be reflected in our measurement of total fertility—
abortions and stillbirths by elongating the intervals between live
births,[10] childbed deaths by the contribution of person-years-lived
to the denominator of our calculations without a birth to augment
the numerator.

The demographic importance of the 1680s becomes clear again
when we push the analysis one step further. The ability of a population to grow by procreation depends on the birth of female
children, for only they can ultimately produce a new generation.
That fact underlies still another statistic, the gross reproduction
rate (GRR), defined as that part of the total fertility rate (TFR)
represented by female births, or

$$(1 \, / \, 2.05) \, * \, TFR.$$

The young females, however, will only contribute to the new generation if they themselves survive to maturity and childbearing, a fact requiring another measure—the net reproduction rate (NRR), or the ratio of the number of females surviving into childbearing to the number of mothers who produced them. Like our other rates, both of these can be expressed in calendar or cohort terms, the former expressing what the ratio would be *if* the conditions prevalent at a given time (the most important of which are those governing mortality) were to remain unchanged. It is this calendar NRR which is so revealing. Given the conditions prevailing between 1650 and 1684, the mothers of Middlesex could produce mothers at a rate of 1.61— that is, given such conditions, each mother of one generation could produce 1.61 mothers in the succeeding generation, implying an intrinsic rate of increase of roughly 10 per 1,000. We gain perspective on this figure by considering that in a representative European population (eighteenth-century Sweden) mothers could reproduce mothers at a rate of 1.07, while in late eighteenth-century New England—in conditions conducive to extraordinary growth—they could do so at a rate of 1.99. In the 1680s in Middlesex, however, changing mortality conditions were such as to drop the net reproduction rate to 1.02. The rate rose from this low to 1.05 in the period 1700–1729. But it did not recover its former level during the period under study.[11] The exact values are, as we have stressed before, less important than the broad suggestion: A relatively vigorous intrinsic rate of growth in Middlesex during the third quarter of the seventeenth century—that is, mothers reproducing themselves and then some—was sharply curtailed in the last quarter of the century and improved only slightly in the first half of the eighteenth.

Let us return to the bar graph of figure 17: Average completed family size. Intuitively this seems the most easily understood of our statistics. If a woman lived throughout her childbearing years, on average she would have roughly seven children.[12] But, of course, not all women lived through their fertile years. Indeed, only a minority did so. Completed family size is not to be confused with the actual number of children born to the average woman of Middlesex. Consider for a moment a woman born in 1690 and acting according to statistical expectation. She would be married at 19 (in 1709) and die at 37 (in 1727). In the course of her life she might be widowed once but in all likelihood would remarry after a year. And

Father's Level	Males		Females	
	Status	Land	Status	Land
Low	23.3	23.7	19.1	19.4
	54	*50*	*75*	*64*
Low Middle	23.8	23.6	20.3	18.9
	21	*26*	*18*	*29*
Middle	23.4	24.3	19.5	19.9
	23	*31*	*15*	*19*
High Middle	22.0	22.7	19.0	19.0
	3	*7*	*2*	*2*
All		23.9		19.3
		120		*116*

Breaking mean age at marriage by the birth order of children suggested no significant differences for either males or females.

4. The sample described in the previous note is free of former servants but not really large enough to support disaggregation by time, as in table 8. The mean age at marriage of 18 native-born males married through 1699 was 23.7, of 72 married 1700–1719 was 23.5, and of 30 married 1720–1750 was 23.9; the mean age at marriage of 33 females married through 1699 was 16.9, of 60 married 1700–1719 was 20.1, and of 22 married 1720–1750 was 21.1.

5. Illegitimacy was, of course, a factor. Births to women with no husbands—a phrase designed to eliminate from consideration premarital pregnancies —constituted 4.5% of all Middlesex births, 1650–1750. The mothers in 40.5% of the cases were servants at the time of the birth, hence the decadal percent of births illegitimate correlates strongly with the percent of the population servant.

6. Our breakdown of survivors differs sharply from the breakdown reported on the basic of Maryland data by Walsh and Menard, "Death in the Chesapeake," *Md. Hist. Mag.*, LXIX (1974), 219, and Menard "Immigrants and Their Increase: The Process of Population Growth in Early Colonial Maryland," Land, et al., eds., *Law, Society and Politics in Early Maryland*, 93–95. Of 362 seventeenth-century Maryland marriages in which the survivor could be identified, 61.0% left a widow, 31.5% a widower, while in 7.5% of the cases husband and wife died within a short time of each other. When we confine our sample to roughly the same parameters—using 634 marriages from the years through 1699—we obtain the following: Wife survived, 40.5%, husband survived, 45.0%, husband and wife died within two years of each other, 14.5%. We suggest that the different results imply no difference in reality but stem from the limitations imposed on Walsh and Menard by the Maryland data base. With inadequate or nonexistent marriage and death records they perforce relied heavily on probate. When we undertake such a count of survivors using only data found in wills we arrive at essentially their results. Thus of 362 Middlesex men who had ever been married and who left wills, 78% left surviving widows, 22% did not. When we go beyond the information in the wills to consider *all* the wives of the 362 men involved—that is, the deceased wives who preceded the surviving wife hence were not mentioned in the wills—we return to our own count. In all the 362 men left 283 living wives but had survived 235 earlier wives who had died; the men had been involved in 597 marriages, 283 (47.4%) of which ended leaving a widow, 314 (52.6%) a widower.

7. The matrix procedure is based upon Barclay, *Population Analysis*, 184–186, the computation of rates on Daniel Scott Smith, "The Demographic History of Colonial New England," *Journal of Economic History*, XXXII (1972), 168–169.

8. The truncation in what follows and in figure 17 is necessitated by weaknesses in our birth data setting in during the late 1740s and increasing over time. The analysis was continued across time to the limit of viability. Even so, we suspect that the last cohort represented on the bar graph and the last point of the line are as much artifacts of weak data as true reflections of conditions. Both points probably dropped in truth, but the drop seems exaggerated.

9. Rutman and Rutman, "Of Agues and Fevers," *WMQ*, 3d Ser., XXXIII (1976), 31–61.

10. But not to the extent that it would create an interval long enough to trigger the automatic assumption of an unrecorded childbirth. We are here referring to the effect of the sum of many small interruptions in the childbearing pattern. Two successive fetal deaths and expulsions three months apart followed by a full-term pregnancy would add six months to what would otherwise be a normal interval, not enough by itself to allow the probability of an intervening and unrecorded birth but enough in an aggregate to affect a summary fertility statistic.

11. The net reproduction rates were computed using the gross reproduction rate and average age of childbearing (T) for a period and, from a lifetable derived as described earlier (under "Mortality") from data on the children born in that period, l[T] / l[0]. This short method of computation follows Smith, "Demographic History of Colonial New England," *Journ. Econ. Hist.*, XXXII(1972), 168–169. The comparative rates are also from Smith. The inclusion of illegitimate births in the analysis would raise the net reproduction rate somewhat for the first and second periods, but only very slightly for the eighteenth century.

12. Recall that the cells of the matrix (figure 16) considered vertically contain the average number of children born to the women of the cohort at the given ages. When we consider the family of the average woman as against the woman with an average completed family—in Middlesex the former dying before achieving the stage of the latter—we must remember that fertility peaks in the early fertile years and declines in the later. Consider the following table of the percent of women bearing one child who went on to have children of a subsequent birth order based upon 114 women alive and under observation throughout their childbearing years:

Birth Order	%	Birth Order	%	Birth Order	%
1	100.0	6	58.6	11	8.1
2	87.9	7	43.4	12	5.1
3	79.8	8	36.4	13	2.0
4	72.7	9	22.2	14	0.0
5	63.6	10	16.2		

If we had 100 women in hand, all of whom had at least one child and lived through their childbearing years, the 100 women would produce 596 children (the sum of the table); if half died following their sixth child, the 100 women would produce 529 children, only 11.2% fewer. Admittedly "the average completed family size of the average woman" is a hybrid number. But it does tend to reflect a real situation.

six

PARENTAL LOSS

In the course of our research on Middlesex the first hint of the extraordinarily high mortality explored earlier came when we began sensing that the loss of one or both parents was a commonplace experience in the lives of children born in the county. Isolated examples—in one instance a sequence of marriages and remarriages involving seven adults and resulting in 25 children, not one of whom could have grown to maturity without losing at least one parent and passing through a period under a stepparent —led us to a formal test of the extensiveness of the phenomenon. The results were presented to a conference on the seventeenth-century Chesapeake held in 1974 and subsequently published in a volume of conference papers.[1]

At the time the test was made our exploitation of Middlesex materials was by no means complete; of necessity we used a rather arbitrarily defined sample, specifically, children born to the wives of men listed on a 1687 militia list for whom we had firm information as to date of birth and parental death dates. With the completion of the biographical data base described in chapter 1 we were in a position to retest the phenomenon using a sample consisting of all children born in the county to 1750. The only restrictions to entry

TABLE 12

Parental Loss in Middlesex,
1650-1750

Achieved Age	N	% Children with Both Parents	% Children with One Parent	% Children Orphaned
		ORIGINAL SAMPLE		
1	239	92.9	7.1	0.0
5	227	76.7	20.7	2.6
9	211	58.8	31.8	9.5
13	194	46.4	34.0	19.6
18	173	32.9	35.8	31.2
*	164	26.8	37.2	36.0
		FULL SAMPLE		
1	1331	93.9	5.6	0.5
5	1246	73.9	22.4	3.7
9	1200	55.1	33.4	11.5
13	1164	40.9	38.2	20.9
18	1125	26.7	39.1	34.2
*	1094	22.6	39.2	38.2

||*Source and Note:* The "Original Sample" is from Darrett B. and Anita H. Rutman, "'Now-Wives and Sons-in-Law': Parental Death in a Seventeenth-Century Virginia County," in Thad W. Tate and David L. Ammerman, eds., *The Chesapeake in the Seventeenth Century: Essays on Anglo-American Society* [Chapel Hill, N.C., 1979], 161. The "Full Sample" is described in the text. An asterisk (*) signifies 21 or age at marriage, whichever came first.

into this larger sample flowed from the nature of the test to be performed: We had to know the age of the child when its parents died, or that the child lived to achieve maturity—defined as age 21 or marriage, whichever came first—with both parents alive. Table 12 depicts the extent of parental loss as originally presented (in the upper segment of the table) and as derived from the full set of Middlesex biographies (in the lower segment). The similarity between the two is gratifying. If anything, our original figures understated the extent of parental loss. Table 13, moreover, shows clearly that the phenomenon of parental loss was a constant over time. By

TABLE 13

Parental Loss in Middlesex
over Time

Ach. Age	Born 1650-1689		Born 1690-1709		Born 1710-1749	
	N	% without One or Both Parents	*N*	% without One or Both Parents	*N*	% without One or Both Parents
1	355	5.9	398	5.3	536	6.3
5	341	26.1	392	27.0	471	24.8
9	330	47.6	388	43.3	441	44.9
13	326	60.7	378	59.5	423	57.2
18	320	76.6	359	73.3	409	70.9
‡	317	77.3	339	79.1	401	76.3

‖*Source and Note:* The table is derived from the sample described in the text. An asterisk (‡) signifies 21 or age at marriage, whichever came first.

way of contrast: In all likelihood only 13 percent of the children of eighteenth-century France were orphaned by age 21—a third the percentage found in Middlesex.[2]

|●|

1. Rutman and Rutman, "'Now-Wives and Sons-in-Law,'" in Tate and Ammerman, eds., *Chesapeake in the Seventeenth Century*, 153-182.

2. Hervé LeBras and Kenneth W. Wachter, "Living Forbears in Stable Populations," in Wachter, et al., *Statistical Studies of Historical Social Structure* (New York, 1978), 163-188.

When all we intend is the delineation of the pool of names from which parents drew, the names alone, grouped by sex, race, and date of entry into or birth in the county constitute our data. A simple frequency count establishes the popularity of particular names, but also the extremely small size of the pool from which white names were drawn. (We will consider black names later.) Tables 14 and 15, for example, isolate the fifteen most popular names among four particular categorizations of white males and females: those entering the county as immigrants in the seventeenth century, and those born in the county in three successive periods. Roughly eight of every ten men in a category and between eight and nine of every ten women bore one of the top fifteen, while between four and five of every ten men and women bore one of the top three—John, William, Thomas among the males; Elizabeth, Mary, Ann among the females. The lists compared to each other (the correlation coefficients entered on the tables) indicate the constancy of the overall pool.

Names rose and fell to some degree in popularity— note the rise of Benjamin from a five-place tie for fifteenth among males born in Middlesex, 1650–1699 to fifth place among the children of 1720–1749. But the pool overall remained largely unchanged. Comparisons between such lists drawn from other areas highlight cultural similarities and divergences. Our Middlesex-born pool originated with the seven-teenth-century immigrants to the county and the immigrant pool was essentially the English pool of the moment. But when the lists are compared to similar lists drawn from New England during the same period the comparison fails. New England, rooted in the Bible, created its own unique pool. John, Thomas, Mary, and Elizabeth remained at or near the top, but for the rest it was a matter of Samuels, Josephs, Joshuas, of Hannahs, Rachels, and Jaels.[3]

To go beyond simply defining the pool of names—that is, to explore for actual patterns in naming—more is required of the data. From our biographies we reconstituted families by linking women to their husbands and children in the same fashion required to study fertility, establishing the age of the mother at each cardinal event (marriage, childbirth) and calculating the intervals between events. And from the set of reconstitutions we selected those capable of bearing the weight of the more stringent analysis of naming patterns. Again, rules: Because, in searching for patterns, we needed to know without doubt the birth order of each child—was it the first son? the third daughter?—we could select only those reconstitutions which contained no intervals between births so large as to hint at a missing child, and only the reconstitutions of first marriages or marriages of individuals whose prior marriages were demonstrably barren. And because we intended probing for generational patterns we could select only those where we knew the names of the parents of both parents, in other words, the maternal and paternal grandparents. The application of the rules to the white population of Middlesex (as reflected in our biographies) gave us in the end a data set of 1,019 children, 563 males and 456 females, grouped in 222 families.[4]

Data on hand, we asked our first question relevant to patterned behavior: How prevalent was name sharing among the children of our families, and particularly between the children of one generation and the preceding generations. Did children tend to bear unique forenames, implying that the culture saw them as unique individuals, or did they share names with parents and grandparents, uncles and aunts, implying that they were construed more as elements of an ongoing family or lineage and less as individuals. William Gray of Middlesex, in his will, reflected the latter view of children. Childless himself, he left his land to his sister Jane's son, Hugh Stewart, on condition "that the said Hugh Stewart Shall Name the first Male Child lawfully begotten of his body Gray Stewart. . . to take up my name on the land." The instances of shared names within our sample immediately suggests that Gray's attitude was general.[5]

Only with respect to their siblings were children individualized. With the exception of necronyms—the names of deceased siblings reused—no two children bore the same forename.[6] For the rest, name-sharing was a common phenomenon. Of male children, 77 percent shared their forename with a father, grandfather, or uncle; 6 percent with some other relation; 3 percent were given the name of

---

||*Source and Notes*: Tables 14 and 15 (following pages) are based on the Middlesex biographies described in chapter 1. The number of cases in the various periods are (males) 1,883, 575, 616, and 839, (females) 676, 560, 555, and 756; total names in the pools (males) 127, 86, 92, and 110, (females) 66, 50, 62, and 58. Duplicate rankings indicate ties. The correlation coefficients (Spearman's *rho* and Pearsonian *r*) are measures of the strength of the relationship between each period and the immediately preceding period, the first period (immigrants) being correlated with Leslie A. Dunkling, *First Names First* (New York, 1977), 76—a compilation of the fifteen most popular baptismal names from 200 English parishes in 1700. In computing *rho*, names appearing on one list and not another are counted as tying for sixteenth place on the latter. Data for computing *r*, the stronger of the two measures, were available only for Middlesex. All correlations are significant at better than a 0.01 level.

TABLE 14

White Male Forenames Found in Middlesex, 1650-1750

White Males Immigrating into Middlesex			White Males Born in Middlesex								
1650-1699			1650-1699			1700-1719			1720-1750		
Rank	Name	Cum %	Rank	Name	Cum %	Rank	Name	Cum %	Rank	Name	Cum %
1	John	19.2	1	John	21.9	1	John	22.9	1	John	19.8
2	Thomas	33.0	2	William	37.2	2	William	38.5	2	William	36.6
3	William	44.7	3	Thomas	49.6	3	Thomas	48.4	3	Thomas	43.7
4	Richard	50.8	4	Richard	54.4	4	James	54.4	4	James	50.5
5	Robert	55.3	5	George	58.8	5	Robert	59.4	5	Benjamin	54.9
6	James	59.5	5	Robert	63.1	6	Henry	64.1	6	George	59.0
7	George	63.0	7	James	67.3	7	Richard	67.2	7	Robert	62.5
8	Edward	66.3	8	Henry	71.3	8	George	69.8	8	Henry	65.4
9	Henry	69.5	9	Charles	73.7	9	Joseph	72.1	9	Samuel	67.8
10	Samuel	71.2	10	Edward	75.3	10	Edward	74.2	10	Charles	70.1
11	Francis	72.5	10	Joseph	76.9	11	Charles	76.0	11	Joseph	72.0
12	Joseph	73.9	12	Peter	78.3	12	Benjamin	77.6	11	Richard	73.9
12	Peter	75.2	12	Samuel	79.3	13	Peter	79.1	13	Daniel	75.4
14	Charles	76.4	14	Francis	80.3	14	Christopher	80.4	13	Edward	76.3
15	Daniel	77.5	15	Benjamin	81.0	15	Daniel	81.3	15	Josiah	77.4
			15	Christopher	81.7	15	Samuel	82.3			
			15	Edmund	82.4						
			15	Nicholas	83.1						
			15	Philip	83.8						
			15	Ralph	84.5						
rho	0.86		0.93			0.90			0.79		
r	n.a.		0.98			0.98			0.97		

TABLE 15.

White Female Forenames Found in Middlesex, 1650-1750

White Females Immigrating into Middlesex 1650-1699			White Females Born in Middlesex								
			1650-1699			1700-1719			1720-1750		
Rank	Name	Cum %	Rank	Name	Cum %	Rank	Name	Cum %	Rank	Name	Cum %
1	Mary	20.1	1	Elizabeth	21.8	1	Mary	16.8	1	Elizabeth	16.5
2	Elizabeth	38.8	2	Mary	37.9	2	Elizabeth	32.3	2	Mary	31.7
3	Ann	52.7	3	Ann	49.8	3	Ann	45.9	3	Ann	45.2
4	Sarah	59.3	4	Sarah	58.6	4	Sarah	54.4	4	Sarah	54.8
5	Margaret	64.5	5	Catherine	64.1	5	Catherine	59.5	5	Jane	60.8
6	Jane	67.9	6	Margaret	68.4	6	Jane	64.3	6	Catherine	66.3
7	Catherine	70.6	7	Frances	72.3	7	Judith	67.9	7	Frances	70.1
8	Frances	73.1	8	Alice	75.0	8	Margaret	71.1	8	Susanna	73.4
9	Alice	75.0	8	Jane	77.7	9	Frances	74.2	9	Judith	76.5
9	Dorothy	76.9	8	Rebecca	80.4	10	Susanna	76.6	10	Margaret	79.0
9	Susanna	78.8	11	Eleanor	82.0	11	Agatha	78.2	11	Lucy	81.3
12	Joan	80.3	12	Lettice	83.4	12	Martha	79.6	12	Ruth	83.1
12	Martha	81.8	13	Hannah	84.6	13	Hannah	80.9	13	Agatha	84.5
14	Hannah	83.1	14	Agatha	85.5	13	Joanna	82.2	14	Avarilla	85.7
15	Rebecca	84.3	14	Judith	86.4	15	Avarilla	83.2	15	Hannah	86.8
			14	Martha	87.3	15	Diana	84.3	15	Rachel	87.8
			14	Mical	88.2						
			14	Winifred	89.1						
rho	0.73			0.70			0.58			0.84	
r	n.a.			0.96			0.94			0.98	

a deceased brother (a necronym); only 14 percent bore unique names. Of females, 69 percent shared a name with a mother, grandmother, or aunt; 6 percent with another relative; 3 percent with a deceased sister; 22 percent with no one. A more refined pattern emerged when we asked the same question of the data broken down by birth order of the children, as in table 16. Roughly 90 percent of the first and second sons shared names with fathers, grandfathers, and uncles as against 40 percent of fifth, sixth, seventh, and eighth sons, more than a third of whom bore unique names. Among daughters the same pattern held, simply to a lesser degree. Some 80 percent of first and second daughters shared names with mothers, grandmothers, aunts;

TABLE 16

Name Sharing by Birth Order in Middlesex,
1650-1750

Birth Order	N	% Sharing Forename with:				
		DS	P,GP	A,U	O	No One
SONS						
1	197	0.0	71.1	17.8	4.6	6.6
2	152	1.3	63.8	26.3	2.6	5.9
3	98	8.2	33.7	30.6	6.1	21.4
4	58	1.7	25.9	36.2	10.3	25.9
5+	58	12.1	13.8	25.9	12.1	36.2
All	563	3.2	52.0	25.0	5.7	14.0
DAUGHTERS						
1	177	0.0	65.5	15.8	1.7	16.9
2	118	1.7	58.5	18.6	6.8	14.4
3	77	5.2	29.9	32.5	5.2	27.3
4	47	10.6	19.1	17.0	21.3	31.9
5+	37	5.4	13.5	27.0	5.4	48.6
All	456	2.9	48.7	20.4	5.9	22.1

‖*Source and Notes:* The table is derived from the sample described in the text. Abbreviations: DS = deceased sibling; P,GP = parent or grandparent; A,U = aunt, uncle; O = other relation. The categories are exclusive from left to right, that is, if a child shares a forename with both a deceased sibling and parent only the first category is augmented, with a parent and uncle or aunt only the second.

less than half the fifth-, sixth-, and seventh-born daughters did so.

Instances of shared names are highly suggestive of a familial rather than individual view of children. But they are not definitive. Consider the case of a father, Thomas, a son John, and a grandson John, with no John among the last John's uncles or on his maternal side. One can presume with small chance of error that the boy was named for his father. But consider another family: Grandfather John and his wife Mary have a son John who marries Ann, daughter of John and Elizabeth and sister of their son John. For whom is John, son of John and Ann, named? His father John? Paternal grandfather John? Maternal grandfather John? Or for his maternal uncle John? To put the question in the truncated but precise vocabulary of this sort of thing, is young John named for his "Fa," "FaFa," "MoFa," or "MoBr"?

There is, of course, no certain answer to such a question. In constructing table 16 we assumed that the cultural norms dictating the naming of children gave precedence to parents and grandparents over aunts and uncles. The resulting symmetry—that is, the rough inverse correlation between the percentages by birth order sharing names with parents and grandparents as opposed to aunts and uncles —tends to validate the assumption. When the precedence is reversed, the symmetry disappears. But the problem of finding the rules of precedence among parents and grandparents, maternal and paternal, remains. Table 17 organizes a subset of the data in such a way as to make apparent a pattern so strong as to make possible a highly probable guess. The table deals solely with first and second sons and daughters who carry the name of either their parent of the same sex or that parent's same-sex parent. Thus, in the male segment of the table, we have included first and second sons who share their forename with either their father or paternal grandfather—54 percent of all first and second sons and 80 percent of all sons bearing the name of a parent or grandparent. In the female segment are all first and second daughters who shared their forename with either their mothers or maternal grandmothers—51 percent of all first and second daughters and 81 percent of all bearing a parent's or grandparent's name. We ignore the far right column of the table. These are instan-- ces such as John son of John naming his son John, or Mary daughter of Mary herself with a daughter Mary. Note, rather, the instances of a child bearing the name of a same-sex parent and *not* that parent's same-sex parent, Fa and not FaFa for example (column 3), and of

TABLE 17

Parents' and Grandparents' Names Shared by
First and Second Sons and Daughters
of Middlesex, 1650–1750

Birth Order	*N*	Subset	% of Column 2 Sharing Name with:		
	(1)	(2)	(3)	(4)	(5)
SONS					
1	197	111	19.8	51.4	28.8
2	152	79	54.4	17.7	27.8
DAUGHTERS					
1	177	92	29.3	63.0	7.6
2	118	57	64.9	26.3	8.8

‖*Source and Notes:* (1) Total number of children from table 16,
which see for source, (2) subset sharing name with a same-sex parent
and/or the same-sex parent of that parent, (3) with same-sex parent
only, (4) same-sex parent's parent only, (5) same-sex parent and
same-sex parent's parent. The table values compute a chi square of
30.17, with 2 degrees of freedom significant at the .001 level—that
is to say, there is a better than 999 out of 1,000 chance of being
correct when we say the table is not the product of purely random
factors.

children bearing the name of the same-sex parent's parent and *not*
the parent, that is FaFa, not Fa (column 4). Note particularly the
reversal of the percentages in these columns between first and second
sons, and that the same reversal occurs in the female segment. These
reversals are improbably the result of chance. The overwhelming
probability is that they are pointing to a pattern of behavior: Parents
tended to name first sons for the child's paternal grandfather, second
sons for the father. Similarly, first daughters tended to be named for
their maternal grandmothers, second daughters for their mothers.[7]

To isolate a central tendency in a society is obviously not to
argue for the inevitability of its operation. The particular naming
pattern we have identified emanated from, and reflects, the strong
family orientation of the society in question. But when we lower
our gaze from the level of the whole society to that of the individual,
personalities and personal situations come into view. By all rights

Richard and Sarah Stevens, both children of a "Sarah," should have
named one of their daughters Sarah. They chose instead "Anne"
(Richard's sister's name) and "Priscilla" (a name unknown in either
family). Why? Conceivably Richard was adamant against the use of
his mother's name; almost immediately after the death of Richard's
father, his mother had been accused before the Middlesex County
Court of "Riotous Liveing" and the "ill Management" of the estate
left in her care.[8] Younger sons conceivably gauged their attachment
to family according to the portion of the family's good's they received.
Charles Wood, the third son of William Wood, is a case in point.
Among the children of his older brothers and sisters were three
Williams, three Janes, three Samuels, and two Catherines—all names
drawn from the family. Additionally, two of the Wood children having
married siblings, each duplicated the siblings' parents' names among
their own children. Charles, however, named his only son for himself,
his first two daughters Sarah and Mary (his wife's mother's name
and wife's name respectively), and, eschewing the Catherine–Jane
syndrome of his own family, named his three other daughters
Elizabeth, Susanna, and Rachel. Richens Brim, another younger son,
eschewed his family's pool of names as well, naming one son for
himself, one for the biblical Melchesedek, and his three daughters
for the daughters of Job: Jemima, Kezia, and Kerenhappuch.

That said we return to the major pattern and the strength of
family which it implies. When the data are disaggregated into cohorts
—as in table 18—the constancy of a concern for family is obvious.
Parents who began childbearing in the seventeenth century drew the
names of their first and second sons from a pool of names defined by
the parents' families of origin (their own parents and their parents'
siblings) roughly 90 percent of the time and the names of their first
and second daughters from the same pool roughly 80 percent of the
time. So too did parents who began childbearing in the years after
1720. Only the proportions drawn from the various parts of the pool
varied, and then only slightly. The clear pattern of first son named
for FaFa, second for Fa (and, on the distaff side, first daughter for
MoMo, second for Mo) is cloudy in the very earliest period, when
the parents were largely immigrants separated by an ocean from their
own parents.[9] Fathers and mothers seem to have loomed larger in the
image of the lineage than did grandparents, symptomatic, perhaps, of
a feeling of a new beginning to the line.[10] And, over time, brothers
and sisters of parents (uncles and aunts of the children) bulked larger

TABLE 18

Name Sharing by First and Second Middlesex Sons
and Daughters by Cohort, 1650-1750

Cohort[*]	N	% Sharing Forename with:			
		P,GP	A,U	O	No One
SONS					
1650-1699	45	73.3	17.8	2.2	6.7
1700-1719	128	68.8	19.5	4.7	6.3
1720-1749	176	65.9	23.9	3.4	6.3
DAUGHTERS					
1650-1699	35	68.6	11.4	2.9	17.1
1700-1719	109	63.3	11.9	4.6	18.3
1720-1749	151	60.9	21.9	3.3	13.9

||*Source and Notes:* The table is derived from the sample described
in the text. See table 16 for abbreviations. Cohort (*) is defined by the
year of birth of the first child in the family, i.e. roughly the equivalent of a marriage cohort. The categories are exclusive from left to right.
The percentage rows do not sum to 100 because of the omission of
necronyms.

as a source of names while parents and grandparents declined, a
function perhaps of a growing awareness of the importance of lateral
kin in the high mortality situation of the Chesapeake.[11]

A complex naming pattern in the Chesapeake involving both
parents and grandparents is, on the surface, a surprising finding
for two reasons. First, the exaggerated mortality of the region can
easily be construed as having worked *against* the pattern. To
whatever extent an expectation of favor might support such patterned
behavior—that is to say, naming a child for a grandparent in the
expectation of the grandparent's favoring the child in a will—to
that extent the pattern was weakened, for in over three-quarters of
the instances of a child named for a grandparent, the grandparent was
dead at the time of the naming. Moreover, the complex skein of marriage and remarriage, its extent a function of mortality, conceivably
worked against adherence to such a naming pattern. We have isolated
that pattern in terms of first marriages; if, indeed, the pattern reflected
a strong cultural trait in the society (and we think it did), then

when we enlarge the scope to encompass second and third marriages
a potential for personal disappointment looms. John Batchelder, son of
William and Sarah, is a case in point. Himself carrying his grandfather's name, he might well have anticipated naming his own sons
William (for FaFa) and John (for Fa). But he married a widow,
Elizabeth (Crank) Davis, who already had among her children a John
and William. Was John disappointed when, barred by the proscriptive
rule against duplicating names among siblings and half-siblings from
naming his first son for either his father or himself, he named the
boy "James" (his brother's name)? To the extent such disappointment
was general the overall pattern would, perhaps, be weakened. But
perhaps not. High mortality could just as easily have strengthened
the family orientation of the society and the naming pattern itself,
the durability of families and lineages contrasting favorably with
the fragility of individual life. And if John Batchelder could not
reproduce by his own seed a William and John, the William and
John who came to him ready-made from Elizabeth's prior marriage
might well have been all the dearer, making a closer family unit out of
the mixed bag of parents, stepparents, siblings, and half-siblings
that, for a while at least, he headed.

A second surprise is the contrast between this Chesapeake
pattern and that isolated for New England by historian Daniel Scott
Smith.[12] Using reconstituted families from Hingham, Massachusetts
for a roughly comparable period, Smith found a significant tendency
to name first-born sons and daughters for the same-sex parent. First
sons shared their father's name in 59.7 percent of his sample, first
daughters their mother's name in 58.6. (The comparable figures from
Middlesex are 27.4 and 19.2 percent respectively.) The parent-grand-
parent syndrome involving first and second sons and daughters is
nowhere in evidence in Hingham. Smith also found that a proscriptive
rule applied not only to siblings but to the children of male patrilineal
cousins, that, for example, two brothers Thomas and William (sons
of Thomas) could not each have a son Thomas. Such was not the
case in Middlesex. In a sample specifically drawn to test for the
phenomenon—73 sets of two or more brothers of a known father,
each brother having sons of his own—names were shared by male
cousins in 63 percent of the sets and by female cousins in 53
percent.[13] The patrilineal grandfather's name (in New England con-
veyed almost exclusively through the eldest son) was, in Middlesex,
shared by coexisting cousins in 42 percent of the 67 sets in which

it occurred at all. The difference hints at a slightly different degree of familial orientation in naming. If, as Smith argues, the extension of the proscriptive rule from siblings to patrilineal cousins indicates a greater individualization of the child, the absence of such extension in the Chesapeake would argue for a higher degree of familialization.

The different patterns found in Middlesex and Hingham become particularly important when we remember that both emerged from still a third pattern—that (or those) prevalent in the English mother culture.[14] The paramount question then becomes the relationship among the three. Does Middlesex reflect more closely traditions of the old country, in which case New England's pattern is a variant? Is New England's pattern in the tradition of the homeland and the Chesapeake's a variant? Or have both overseas areas varied from the original? Assume for a moment the first question is answered affirmatively; one could then argue that, in New England, the force of a Puritan ideology and the accent within that ideology of the role of the father as governor of the family had a direct effect upon behavior. Assume that the first is answered negatively and the second affirmatively—the Middlesex pattern is the variant. One could argue that the variation flowed from the high mortality of the early Chesapeake.

We make no conclusive choice between these two alternatives. True, New England differed from old England in the biblicism of its names, but this is not necessarily a telling point when it comes to the naming pattern itself. The choice must depend upon what pattern (or patterns) prevailed in England and to the best of our knowledge the requisite studies have not been made. We simply offer a hint in table 19. The table contrasts results from both our Middlesex sample and Smith's Hingham sample with those from an availability sample drawn from licenses to leave England for the colonies in the 1630s.[15] Some of these licenses—all involving departures for New England— include the names and ages of parents and their English-born and English-named children, hence approximate English family reconstitutions. Obviously important data are missing. We have no idea of grandparents. We can work safely only with the first sons and daughters listed, and only then when the parents' and childrens' ages are such as to allow an assumption that the children are indeed the first born of their sex. Equally obvious is the potential for bias in the data. All the families were underway for Puritan New England; if they were English Puritans they could already be naming

TABLE 19

Percentage of First Children Sharing Name with Same-Sex
Parent in Middlesex, Hingham, Mass., and in English
Families Immigrating to New England

Sample	Sons		Daughters	
	N	*%*	*N*	*%*
Middlesex 1650-1750	197	27.4	177	19.2
English Immigrant Families To N.E.	71	28.2	61	19.7
Hingham 1640-1760	385	59.7	408	58.6

‖*Source:* The Middlesex data are described in the text, English immigrants to New England have been compiled from John Camden Hotten,
ed., *The Original Lists of Persons . . . Who Went From
Great Britain to the American Plantations, 1600-1700*
(London, 1874), Hingham data from Daniel Scott Smith, "Child-Naming
Patterns and Family Structure Change: Hingham, Massachusetts,
1640-1880," *The Newberry Papers in Family and Community History*, no. 76-5 (1977).

children according to a variant pattern which would ultimately prevail in New England and be isolated by Smith. In any event, the
results are startling for the similarity between English immigrants
and Middlesex and for the contrast of both with Smith's Hingham
findings. The table, in brief, suggests that New England's naming
pattern was the variant.

Our excursion into the naming of children in Middlesex offers
two other suggestions as to the nature of Chesapeake society. First,
when names were not drawn from a family pool, what sorts of names
were selected? Trends in such freely chosen names have long been
suspected of reflecting broad cultural trends; the English reforma-
tion, for example, brought with it a radical shift from traditional
names with roots in the non-biblical saints—Agatha, for example—to
biblical and particularly Old Testament names such as Sarah. These
shifts are not readily caught, however. Simply counting names (as
in tables 14 and 15) and categorizing them as biblical or non-biblical,

TABLE 20

Biblical and Secular Names among Freely Chosen
(Non-Familial) Names in Middlesex, 1650-1750

Year of Birth	N	% Biblical	% Secular
1650-1709	23	39.1	60.9
1710-1749	47	68.1	31.9
All	70	58.6	41.4

||*Sources and Notes:* See text for the derivation of the
sample. The determination of biblical and secular has been made
using George R. Stewart, *American Given Names: Their
Origin and History in the Context of the English
Language* (New York, 1979), E. G. Withycombe, *The Oxford
Dictionary of English Christian Names*, (3d edn.,
Oxford, 1977), and Leslie A. Dunkling, *First Names First*
New York, 1977). Sample size precludes disaggregation into any
finer periods or by sex.

although easy to do, is not definitive for it fails to take into
account the fact that in a situation dominated by a family-oriented
naming pattern, a freely-chosen name quickly moves into the family
pool and recurs not as an example of free choice but by virtue of
the family-oriented pattern. In Middlesex "Kezia" is a case in point.
Arriving in the county in 1685 in the person of Keziah (or Kezia)
Ball, the name occurs time and again in the generations descended
from her but only once to 1750 in an unrelated individual. Clearly
we cannot simply count all "Kezias" in an effort to determine the
biblical orientation of the culture. By this reasoning, the rise of
Benjamin in table 14 and the appearance of Josiah in the last
grouping there can only be taken as hints of an increasing biblicism
in Middlesex to be confirmed or refused by a more refined procedure.
Our way has been to have recourse to our more stringently derived
sample to count and categorize only *unique* names, that is, names
which are *not* found within the family pool associated with the
parents. The penalty for this procedure is a small sample but the
benefit is a sample devoid of family bias. Table 20 depicts the
results. The overall extent to which biblical names were resorted to
in situations of free choice (almost 60 percent of all cases) is
surprising. Smith, counting *all* Hingham names for a comparable

period, found 85 percent biblical.[16] Even more revealing, however,
is the shift over time from a secular to biblical orientation, confirming to an extent the hint offered by the rise of Benjamin.

Thus far all of our findings refer to Middlesex's white population.
What of its blacks? Blacks were present from the first settlement of
the county in 1650. In the 1680s and 1690s Africans began arriving in
larger and larger numbers as slavery displaced white servitude. By
the 1720s, as we have seen, a majority of the county's population
was black. And roughly a quarter of the entries in our Middlesex
data file are of blacks. What do their names tell us?

The question is particularly pertinent in the light of work of the
last few years. Scholars intent on reconstructing the culture of the
slaves (and accentuating African elements in the doing) have tended
to stress the African names among the slaves—the Cuffees and Jubas
—and the appearance of days of the week as names, reflecting a
common African practice of giving children the name of the day on
which they were born. In the hands of these scholars the naming of a
newly arrived slave is made into a bargain between the white master
and the black slave, the latter struggling to retain his or her own name
and identity. Thus Jack is accepted (and John presumably rejected)
because Jack sounds like Quaco (Wednesday), Jemmy is accepted in
lieu of James because of the former's likeness to Quame (Saturday),
Abby rather than Abigail because it sounds like Abba (Thursday).
In this interpretation the names proferred and accepted became the
pool of black names from which slave parents drew in naming their
own children according to a pattern carried from Africa or derived
within the condition of slavery.[17]

What does our Middlesex data offer?

||*Source and Notes*: Tables 21 and 22 (following pages) are based on the Middlesex
biographies described in chapter 1. The number of cases in the various periods are
(males) 139, 433, 662, and 456, (females) 131, 445, 665, and 496, total names in the pools
(males) 127, 86, 92, and 110, (females) 39, 71, 85, 78. Only the most frequent variant is listed.
For example, given 19 Wills, 13 Billys, 2 Williams, and 1 Bill, we list only Will. In
addition to the three formal male names for which there were no diminutives (Peter,
George, Charles), formal names accounted for only 4.4% of the entire male sample.
The percentage was highest among those entering 1650–1699 (8.6%). See tables 14 and
15 for definitions of *r* and *rho*. Correlations are computed (1) between each period and
the period immediately preceding it, and (2) between each period and white names of the
same sex born in Middlesex during the same period. All correlations are significant at
better than a 0.01 level.

TABLE 21

Black Male Forenames Found in Middlesex, 1650-1750

| | Entering or Born in Middlesex | | | | | | Born in Middlesex 1720-1750 | | | Entering Middlesex 1720-1750 | | |
| | 1650-1699 | | | 1700-1719 | | | | | | | | |
Rank	Name	Cum %	Rank	Name	Cum %	Rank	Name	Cum %	Rank	Name	Cum %
1	Jack	10.8	1	Jack	11.8	1	Will	6.5	1	Jack	7.5
2	Will	18.7	2	Will	19.9	2	Jack	11.9	2	Harry	13.2
2	Peter	26.6	3	Tom	26.1	3	Jemmy	16.8	3	Will	18.4
4	Tom	33.1	4	Tony	31.6	3	Peter	21.6	4	Dick	23.0
5	Dick	38.8	5	Dick	36.3	5	Tom	26.3	4	Sam	27.6
5	Harry	44.6	5	Harry	40.9	6	Harry	30.7	6	Jemmy	32.0
7	James	49.6	7	Robin	44.6	7	Ben	34.6	6	Tom	36.4
7	Tony	54.7	8	Peter	48.0	8	Dick	38.4	8	Robin	40.3
9	Frank	59.0	9	Ben	51.3	9	Robin	41.7	9	Peter	43.9
10	George	62.6	10	George	54.0	10	Tony	44.9	10	George	47.1
10	Ned	66.2	11	Frank	56.4	10	Charles	48.0	11	Tony	49.6
12	Ben	69.1	12	Jemmy	58.4	12	Sam	50.9	12	Charles	51.8
12	Sambo	71.9	12	Sam	60.5	13	George	53.5	13	Ben	53.7
12	Samson	74.8	14	Cesar	62.4	14	Ned	55.6	14	Cesar	55.0
12	Robin	77.7	14	Ned	64.2	15	Mingo	57.6	14	Sawney	56.4
							Phil	59.5			
rho [1]	–			0.76			0.72			0.78	
[2]	0.60			0.53			0.63			0.63	
r [1]	–			0.92			0.92			0.79	
[2]	0.74			0.86			0.70			0.70	

98

TABLE 22

Black Female Forenames Found in Middlesex, 1650-1750

	Entering or Born in Middlesex						Born in Middlesex 1720-1750			Entering Middlesex 1720-1750		
	1650-1699			1700-1719								
Rank	Name	Cum %	Rank	Name	Cum %	Rank	Name	Cum %	Rank	Name	Cum %	
1	Betty	15.3	1	Betty	8.3	1	Jenny	6.2	1	Jenny	8.5	
2	Moll	26.0	2	Jenny	16.0	2	Moll	12.2	2	Kate	15.5	
3	Kate	32.8	3	Moll	23.4	3	Judy	17.9	3	Bess	21.6	
4	Jenny	38.9	3	Sarah	30.8	4	Frank	23.3	4	Moll	27.4	
4	Nanny	45.0	5	Kate	37.8	4	Nan	28.7	5	Judy	33.1	
6	Pegg	49.6	6	Frank	43.8	6	Kate	33.5	6	Beck	38.3	
7	Frank	54.2	7	Judy	49.4	6	Sarah	38.3	7	Nan	42.9	
8	Joan	58.0	8	Sue	54.2	8	Betty	42.7	8	Dinah	46.9	
8	Sarah	61.8	9	Dinah	58.2	8	Hannah	47.1	8	Frank	50.8	
10	Judith	64.9	10	Phillis	61.6	10	Lucy	50.8	8	Sarah	55.0	
10	Phillis	67.9	11	Hannah	64.7	11	Dinah	54.4	11	Hannah	58.7	
12	Alice	70.2	11	Nanny	67.9	12	Phillis	57.9	11	Phillis	62.2	
12	Hannah	72.5	13	Letty	70.8	13	Letty	61.1	13	Peg	65.3	
12	Nora	74.8	13	Rose	73.7	14	Margery	63.9	14	Lucy	67.5	
12	Sue	77.1	15	Alice	76.4	15	Rose	66.3	15	Sue	70.8	
rho [1]	-			0.56			0.65			0.69		
[2]	0.65			0.62			0.61			0.63		
r [1]	-			0.62			0.61			0.54		
[2]	0.90			0.60			0.56			0.49		

The first argument—strained at best—is simply untenable. On the one hand, we found among 3,429 slaves entering or born in Middlesex prior to 1750 only 23 day names in either an African or English form —a little over one-half of one percent—and fewer than 150 African names in all (4.4%) even when taking the liberty of construing every strange appearing name "African." On the other hand, we found a significant correlation between the white names in common use (tables 14 and 15) and their diminutive or, more properly, familial forms among the blacks (tables 21 and 22). Bargains were undoubtedly struck at times—historian Peter Wood recounts one slave's narrative of a futile attempt to bargain[18]—and African names were occasionally accepted by whites. But when the aggregate is considered it is clear that the initial pool of black names (at least in Middlesex) was established by whites assigning familial forms of common English names.

That such should be the case is quite understandable when we realize the ways in which names were used in the white society. As historians we come to know, and consequently to identify, the whites solely by their formal names. But this is simply a function of the way in which we gain our knowledge. Our sources almost inevitably reflect formal occasions. In baptismal records, legal appearances, contracts, and the like people's names were set down (for us to read) as Matthew, Francis, Henry, Mary, Susanna. Yet these same people bore familial names and now and again the records allow us to see their use on informal occasions: "Matt" Kemp, "Frank" Dodson, "Harry" Daniell, "Poll" Cole, "Molly" Byrd, "Sukey" Carter. Once in a very great while the records allow us to see the relationship between the particular form of the name as used and the relative situations of the individuals using it—the snippet of conversation recorded as part of a lawsuit which we have used on several occasions in the primary volume of this work, for example. The speakers are Alice Creyke and Jane Olney, women of very different social standing; the subject of their conversation is Richard Gabriell, Creyke's servant. Jane speaks first:

[I] Asked, "Madam, I pray Madam, why are you in such Anger and bitterness against me?"

"Jane, not I. But you meddle with Dick the Taylor my Servant. . . and threaten to take away his Eares."

"Truly Madam, Not I if I can help it. . . . I shall not meddle with Richard nor any that belongs to you."[19]

As we argued in the primary volume, different social positions in part determined the form of address—Mistress Olney speaking upward to "Madam," Madam speaking downward to "Jane." But the familial position of Gabriell relative to the speakers was also determinative. He was Madam's servant and construed a dependent within the family, in effect akin to a child, hence Madam referred to "Dick"; he was a person apart from the Olney family, hence Jane referred to "Richard." Slavery being rationalized in familial terms—William Byrd's strolling his plantation, viewing his "family" at work comes to mind—the assignment of the familial form of English names to the blacks naturally followed.[20] And because the slave had no existence apart from the family, he or she had nothing but a familial name, just as he or she had no surname. To everyone and on every occasion a particular slave would be simply Madam Creyke's Jack.

Of the second argument—the assignment of names to black children by their parents in some patterned way—we can speak only tangentially. In order to test for the existence of such patterned behavior and have any measure of confidence in the results, we need the sort of carefully derived data which we used in discerning patterns among the whites. We simply do not have them. It is, indeed, appropriate to ask if a slave bore his father's name? his grandfather's? his paternal uncle's? But it would be irresponsible to attempt an answer when we know the names of fathers in only a handful of cases. We know more frequently the child's mother. But this suggests only a negative. Few black girls—not even enough to allow us to argue for more than a random coincidence—bore their mother's name.

Our black name lists (tables 21 and 22) suggest another negative. The existence of a strong naming pattern in a population will inevitably tend to reinforce the popularity of leading names within the pool. The complex mathematics of this phenomenon can be demonstrated in a crude way by tracking the names of the male descendants of John, son of Thomas, in a culture in which the following hierarchial rules are invariant: (1) Every first son is to be named for his paternal grandfather; (2) every second son for his father; (3) no two sons of a father can bear the same name; (4) wherever possible the name of a father's brother must be used. If we assume that every male has but two sons the pool will never grow beyond John and Thomas. If we reverse the fourth rule to make it proscriptive—the name of a father's brother is never to be used—and so force the introduction of new names, our pool in four generations will still be dominated by John and Thomas (50%). The tabulation of white names (tables 14 and 15) demonstrates the phenomenon in reality for note the consistent strength of the top four male and female names, encompassing in every group over fifty percent of all cases. But the top four black names, male and female, among Middlesex-born blacks, 1720–1749 account for less than half this number.[21] Note, too, that 1,595 Middlesex-born white children, 1720–1749 shared 168 names, a ratio of 9.5 to 1; 1,327 black children born in the same period shared 219 names (6 to 1). The mere size of the black pool argues against strongly patterned behavior.

Beyond such negative arguments, however, we can question for this early period the basic assumption that underlies the very notion of a pattern, that is, that slave parents themselves assigned their children's names. Consider, for example, William Stanard's slaves. Between 1717 and 1729, in conformity with the requirements of the law, he brought ten imported black children into the Middlesex County Court to have their ages adjudged. Stanard was obviously intrigued with the classics for the children's names were given as Pompey, Scipio, Bacchus, Cesar, Cupid, Julius, Jupiter, Mars, and—apparently momentarily at a loss—Orronoco (a variety of tobacco) and Sommerset. Between 1715 and 1728 he registered sixteen children born to his slaves: Apollo, Letty, Clarinda, Molly, Cyrus, Mercury, Frank, Phillis, Titan, Jerrell, Irene, London, Juno, Winny, Nimrod, and Diana. At least in this case it seems obvious who was choosing the names of the children born on the plantation. A more general clue lies in what we term the "Lucy Syndrome." Through 1719 only a handful of white Lucys appear in Middlesex—four entering from England, one native-born; after 1720, however, the popularity of the name surged and it moved into eleventh place among the whites. Black Lucys followed the same trend, from a sprinkling through 1719 to tenth place among native-born blacks, 1720–1749. Still another clue lies in the makeup of particular slave holdings. We found no instance of Middlesex-born blacks of the same generation bearing exactly the same name on the same plantation. In every case an apparent violation of this finding proved to be a matter of either a predeceased child of the same generation or a black purchased or inherited already bearing the name of a slave on the plantation. In the latter instance some sort of modifier was almost invariably added to the name of one or the other of the slaves—"Jack Rascow" (rascal?), for example, or

"Barbary Jack," or "Jack Carpenter." In the same way modifiers were used on the relatively rare occasions of intergenerational name duplication (rare because of high mortality): "Great Alice" and "Little Alice," "Old Doll" and "Doll."

None of this is meant to argue that blacks played absolutely no role in the naming of their children, only that at this time in Middle-sex the necessity of the white owner being able to delineate between hands was a sharp constraint on the development of indigenous naming. Should William Stanard send for "Young Molly" he could not countenance his messenger asking "which one?" In this situation the most that one might expect is that black parents put forward a name for their newborn child to be accepted or rejected by the white master.[22]

Neither is this to argue a unique conclusion. In an analysis of nineteenth century black names published in the 1930s—an aggregative analysis and hence comparable to our own as the recent qualitative, that is to say, selective, studies are not—the investigator discerned "the direct or indirect influence of the master in the naming of the slave child" and diminutives following "patterns current in the white population." "Slave children," he concluded, "were often, if not usually, actually named by the master or mistress."[23]

|●|

1. *The Tragedy of Romeo and Juliet*. Act II. Scene ii, James Joyce, *Ulysses* (Random House ed., [New York, 1946]), 207.

2. Daniel Scott Smith, "Child-Naming Patterns and Family Structure Change: Hingham, Massachusetts 1640–1880," *The Newberry Papers in Family and Community History*, no. 76–5 (1977), 2–4 briefly reviews the theoretical basis for linking discernible naming patterns and culture. Smith's work proceeded from studies in anthropology, sociology, and geography, notably Claude Lévi-Strauss, *The Savage Mind* (Chicago, 1966); Alice S. Rossi, "Naming Children in Middle Class Families," *American Sociological Review*, 30 (1965), 499–513; Wilbur Zelinski, "Cultural Variation in Personal Name Patterns in the Eastern United States," *Annals of the Association of American Geographers*, 60 (1970), 743–769. Despite the fact that it has been available since first presented in 1972 at a Clark University Conference on the Family and Social Structure, Smith's study has not been systematically replicated by Americanists nor have any efforts been made to extend the analytic device or findings. Early American historians, for example, have been content to offer snippets couched in Smithian terms. Continental scholarship (but not British) is well advanced. Note in *L'Homme: Revue Française d'Anthropologie* 20 (1980), the entire fall

issue devoted to the subject of names.

3. See Leslie A. Dunkling, *First Names First* (New York, 1977), 76 for the English list, Daniel Scott Smith, "Child-Naming Practices as Cultural and Familial Indicators," forthcoming, for the New England list. We are grateful to Professor Smith for allowing us access to his count before publication. Rank-order correlations between Middlesex and the New England the lists supplied by Smith are in the order of 0.01 to 0.25.

4. The skewed sex ratio in the sample (123 males per 100 females) is an artifact of the procedure. An "under-registration" of females and the genetic element in sex-determination combine to create a bias against families inclined to female births and toward those inclined to males. The bias does not affect the analysis here.

5. Middlesex Wills, 1713-1734, 374. In what follows, the construction of a forename from a surname has been accounted an instance of name-sharing. Middle names were all but unknown in early Middlesex. There were only four in the refined data set, all male.

6. The proscriptive rule by which children were individualized with reference to siblings extended across multiple marriages. We have noted only one clear instance in all our Middlesex data in which it was broken. Among the children of Penelope Paine by two husbands were her first son Thomas (by Thomas Warwick) and fifth son Thomas (by William Cheyney), the first son Thomas was alive at the time the second was born and subsequently named his first daughter Penelope. In another case, William Hackney, who had 14 children by two wives, named his third and seventh daughters Sarah and Sally respectively, but this seems an early example of "Sally's" gradual emergence as a name independent of its origin.

7. The significance of the grandparent in the pattern shows again in necronyms, 42% of which were apparently efforts to retain the forename of a grandparent, 26% attempts to retain the forename of a parent.

8. Middlesex Wills, 1698-1713, 179; Orders, 1705-1710, 27.

9. When table 17 is regenerated by cohort, the seventeenth-century cohort varies sharply from the general pattern. Of seventeenth-century first sons bearing the name of Fa and/or FaFa, 50% are instances of Fa not FaFa, 12.5% of FaFa not Fa, of first daughters bearing the name of Mo and/or MoMo, 64% are instances of Mo not MoMo, 27% MoMo not Mo. The pattern displayed in eighteenth-century cohorts are simply random variants of each other and of the pattern indicated in table 18.

10. Daniel Blake Smith, *Inside the Great House: Planter Family Life in Eighteenth Century Chesapeake Society* (Ithaca, N.Y., 1980) 229 and *n*, catches a glimpse of this phenomenon but his analysis is too rudimentary to allow real comparison.

11. When the basic first son for FaFa, second son for Fa rule was violated, the name given the child was more often than not one shared with one of the father's male siblings or a relative in the maternal line (MoFa, MoBr), in such instances there seems to have been a tendency, particularly in the case of first sons, to link the child to *both* lines—for example, select a name common to both FaBr and MoFa or FaBr and MoBr. Such duplication occurred in the case of 19% of first sons sharing a name with FaBr, MoBr, and/or MoFa, 10% of second sons, and 4% of 3rd through 8th sons, in 19% of the instances of a first daughter sharing a name with MoSi, FaSi, and/or MoMo, 15% of such second daughters, and 2% of 3rd through 7th daughters. Such behavior would be logical in a high mortality situation where orphaned children were common. Notably,

orphaned elder children would be more in need of kin-protection than orphaned younger children who would have elder siblings.

12. Smith, "Child-Naming Patterns," *Newberry Papers*, no. 76-5 (1977), passim.

13. The original sample contained too few brothers to make the test. The larger sample was created by dropping the rule that we must know the name of the mother and maternal grandmother of the children.

14. To speak of *an* English pattern—singular—is, at this point in time, merely a convenience. It is certainly possible that there were *many* English patterns. It is also possible that there was an overarching *western* concern (although not a single, precise pattern) to link children to the lineage by keeping alive the name of grandparents. Christiane Klapisch-Zuber, "L'Attribution d'un Prénom a L'Enfant en Toscane a la Fin du Moyen-Age," *L'Enfant au Moyen-Age*, Publications du CUER MA, Université de Provence, 9 (Aix-En-Provence, 1980), 75–84, her "Le Nom 'Refait': La Transmission des Prénoms à Florence (XIVe-XVIe Siècles), *L'Homme*, 20 (1980), 77-104, André Burguière's "Un Nom Pour Soi: Le Choix Nom de Baptême en France Sous l'Ancien Régime" in the same journal, pp. 25–42, and Nicholas Tavuchis, "Naming Patterns and Kinship Among Greeks," *Ethnos*, 36 (1971), 152-162, are suggestive. The Chesapeake naming pattern clearly reflects such a concern.

15. As printed in John Camden Hotten, ed., *The Original Lists of Persons. . . Who Went From Great Britain To the American Plantations. 1600-1700* (London, 1874).

16. In the original paper as presented in 1972 (see note 2) and cited with permission of the author. See also David W. Dumas, "The Naming of Children in New England, 1780-1850," *The New England Historical and Genealogical Register*, 132 (1978), 196-210.

17. See for example J. L. Dillard, *Black English: Its History and Usage in the United States* (New York, 1972), 123–135; Eugene Genovese, *Roll, Jordan, Roll: The World the Slaves Made* (New York, 1972), 447-450; Peter H. Wood, *Black Majority: Negroes in Colonial South Carolina from 1670 through the Stono Rebellion* (New York, 1974), 181-186, P. Robert Paustian, "The Evolution of Personal Naming Practices Among American Blacks," *Names* 26 (1978), 177-191, Cheryll Ann Cody, "Naming, Kinship and Estate Dispersal: Notes on Slave Family Life on a South Carolina Plantation, 1786 to 1833," *WMQ*, 3d Ser., 39 (1982), 198-206. Notably Newbell Niles Puckett's work—inevitably cited—supports none of this, although his "Names of American Negro Slaves," *Studies in the Science of Society*, ed. George Peter Murdock (New Haven, 1937), 477-490 was the only analysis of a large aggregation of black names (10,954, largely from Mississippi) available when these authors were writing.

18. Wood, *Black Majority*, 181-182n.

19. Middlesex Deeds, 1679-1694, 31.

20. Louis B. Wright and Marion Tinling, eds., *The Secret Diary of William Byrd of Westover. 1709-1712* (Richmond, Va., 1941), 19, 34, 483. See also Peter Laslett, *The World we have lost*, 1-15; Gerald W. Mullins, *Flight and Rebellion: Slave Resistance in Eighteenth-Century Virginia* (New York, 1972), 3-33. Among whites familial names occasionally trespassed into the realm of formal names in the seventeenth century but they did so increasingly in the eighteenth—Betty as a baptismal name, for example, perhaps it was an ironic consequence of the fact that

with slavery the familial forms were so much more publicly expressed.

21.   Note, too, the diffusion of names where patterned behavior is considered weak to non-existent in Kenneth M. Weiss, et al., "Wherefore Art Thou, Romio? Name Frequency Patterns and their Use in Automated Genealogy Assembly," *Genealogical Demography*, ed. Bennett Dyke and Warren T. Morrill (New York, 1980), 52, 57, and Dunkling, *First Names First*, 17, usage of the top four names ranges from roughly 13 to 17%, of the top ten from 26 to 33%.

22.   There are hints that when blacks assumed a significant role in naming their children they patterned their behavior on the whites. Mary Beth Norton, in a brief analysis of child-naming among Thomas Jefferson's slaves, 1774-1822, noted that "black youngsters who bore their grandparents' names held a marked percentage edge over their parentally named siblings (57 percent to 43 percent)." *Liberty's Daughters: The Revolutionary Experience of American Women, 1750-1800* (Boston, 1980), 85-87. Norton's analysis is not such as to allow a definitive statement, but it looks very much like Jefferson's slaves were following our grandfather pattern in naming their children. Cf., however, Herbert G. Gutman, *The Black Family in Slavery and Freedom, 1750-1925* (New York, 1976), 186-199.

23.   Puckett, "Names of American Negro Slaves," *Science of Society*, ed. Murdock, 489.

eight

SOCIAL NETWORKS

The analysis of kinship and friendship underlying the conclusions of chapter 4 is based upon our computerized biographies of 12,215 residents of Middlesex.[1] Our knowledge of kin and affinal relationships flowed from our knowledge of parentage and marriage. If two men had the same father and mother they were clearly brothers; if they married sisters, they were also brothers-in-law. The search for relationships was entirely a computer operation. The package of search routines developed for the purpose was modeled roughly after that written by anthropologist George A. Collier of Stanford University and can isolate a relationship as remote from a subject as a spouse's great-grandmother's sister's great-granddaughter—an affinal third cousin.[2] Obviously, however, the ability to isolate such a remote connection does not mean that the relationship was meaningful; in actual practice the search stopped long before reaching this extreme.

What we refer to as friendship connections are quite different from kin and affinal relationships, although ultimately we tested for overlap between the two. In a few cases we knew of friendship directly—when, for example, one individual referred to another as "friend." But for the most part we had to infer friendship from legal documents. Our way was, first, to isolate all appearances of individuals as witnesses, securities, guardians, attorneys, godparents, and the like, then search for signs of socially reciprocal behavior between individuals or within groups. If, for example, an individual stood security for another and the second subsequently gave bond for the guardianship of the orphaned children of the first, we assumed friendship between the two. Similarly, if an individual repeatedly served as a witness to documents in consort with other socially cooperating individuals, or repeatedly and reciprocally served in such a capacity for a single individual, we presumed friendship. Always, however, we ignored strictly economic relationships, isolated occurrences, and all occurrences within a context suggestive more of a "patron-client" relationship than of friendship—in chapter 4, for example, the appearance as witnesses to the will of Andrew Williamson of Richard Robinson, Robinson's clerk, and a professional attorney frequently associated with Robinson.[3]

The data within which we searched for kinship and friendship are obviously incomplete. We do not know parentage in many cases, while the acronym for an unknown spouse—"LNU, FNU," that is, "Last Name Unknown, First Name Unknown"—appears all too frequently. And friendship certainly existed, particularly between women, without leaving evidence in our materials. What data we have are also biased. We are, for example, much more likely to have parentage and marriages for people born in the county than for those immigrating and more friendships for the long-lived active male than for the short-lived or relatively inactive. The important point, however, is that what we know is always minimal. We know a given individual is related to *at least* "x" number of individuals and probably has *at least* "x" number of friends; he could be related to more and could have additional friends. Numbers derived by aggregating such cases are, consequently, themselves minimal, important as such and for the trends they show.

Our analysis of friendship and kinship was keyed on individuals appearing as household heads in censuses reconstructed for 1687, 1704, and 1724.[4] Our specific question was: To what other heads of household was any particular head related in the year of the census in question? Logic and practical considerations dictated this strategy. Theoretically we could have searched for the kin and friends of each of the 12,215 persons in the data set at any or all points

in time. Practically we could not. Even the most modern high-speed computer requires time to undertake a search, and the computer's time is money. As it was, compiling the relationships and cross-linkages of some 250 to 300 people at each of three points in time required more than 25 minutes of central processing time and 30 hours of real time. To this must be added the time required of the authors to make certain subjective judgments about friendships and additional computer time to analyze the results. Limiting the work to census years made the project manageable. The three particular censuses were chosen by a process of elimination. Of the six available, those of 1668 and 1740 were eliminated because of weaknesses in the data. There is a complete hiatus in county records between the formation of Middlesex and the early 1670s, while only a scattering of marriage records exist from the late 1730s onward. The censuses of 1699 and 1704 were so close together as to make a search for relationships keyed on both redundant. The latter was chosen as the stronger of the two. Finally, the limitation to household heads followed from the logical proposition that a relationship between heads implies to some extent a relationship between members of their households. Obviously the children of brothers (both household heads) would be related as cousins, but even a simple friendship between heads implies some sort of tie between their children.

The results of our search for relationships are presented in the accompanying figures and tables. The first (figure 18) depicts for each census the percentage of all household heads related by friendship and kinship separately to (1) no other head, (2) between one and four heads, and (3) five or more heads. The steadily enlarging kinship networks suggested by the lower diagram is to be expected. Men and women entered the county, married, and had children and grandchildren who in turn married, steadily expanding the number of ties between families as a simple function of time. Yet note the constant level of friendship suggested in the upper diagram and again in figure 19. When, in figure 20, the data are disaggregated on the basis of status groups (as defined infra) it becomes clear that status and the number of kinship and friendship links are related. But while mean kinship links swell for household heads in every status group, mean friendship links (although increasing with status) remain fairly constant across time.[5]

Expanding kinship and a constant level of friendship are suggested again by formal correlation. Immigrants to Middlesex, on the one hand, had appreciably fewer kin connections than did those born in the county, with place of birth accounting for 24 percent of the variation in the number of kinship links. On the other hand, immigrants and native-born had roughly the same number of friendships, and place of birth accounted for only 2.4 percent of the variation.[6] Table 23, too, reveals expanding kinship (column 3) and a constant level of friendship (column 4), with an added phenomenon suggested in the last column. When kin were relatively few in number, friends were largely unrelated (85 percent in 1687), but as kin became more common individuals tended to rely more on them as friends and less

FIGURE 19

Middlesex Household Heads by the Number of Other
Heads to Which Each Was Linked by Friendship,
1687, 1704, 1724.

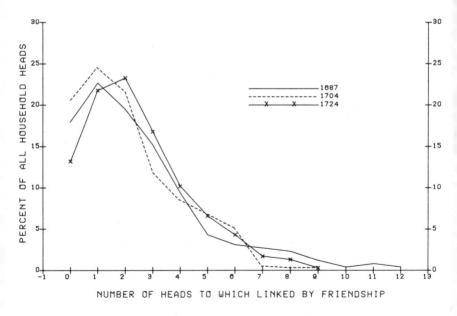

‖*Source and Note:* See text for source. *N*, mean, median and standard deviation for each census: (1687) 256, 2.5, 2.0, 0.15; (1704) 296, 2.1, 1.7, 0.1; (1724) 303, 2.4, 2.1, 0.1.

FIGURE 20

Mean Friendship and Kinship Links of Middlesex Householders
to Other Household Heads by Status and Time

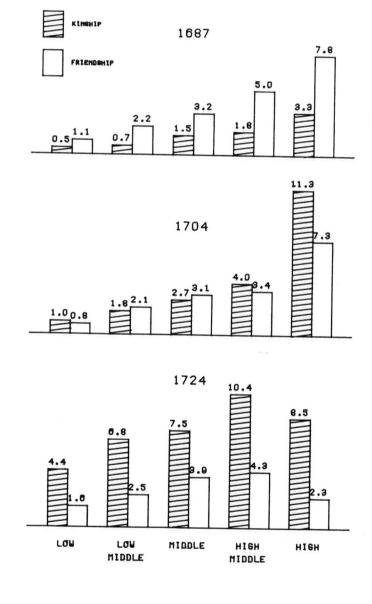

on unrelated neighbors (50 percent of the friends of 1724 were unrelated). Finally, table 24 suggests a real application of friendship and kinship. In the earliest period (1650–1689) roughly half of all guardians having charge of an orphan in the county were related to their wards (23 percent as aunt or uncle); in the last period (1720–1750) the percentage of related guardians rose to 66 percent (50 percent related as aunt or uncle).

That kinship would grow while the number of friends remained constant is eminently logical. The former, as has been said, is inevitably a function of marriage, reproduction, and, ultimately, time. The latter, it can be argued, is a social necessity—people inevitably need others on whom they can rely—but is subject to an inherent limitation. Those reciprocal relationships which we call friendship require from us both our time and our concern, yet there is only so much time in a day, week, or month, and only so much of ourselves that can be spared for others. Thus, while the potential for kinship is infinite, the number of friends is finite. Such considerations ought to put us on guard against the too facile dismissal of support networks in the seventeenth century and too ready acceptance of the notion that a plethora of kin in the eighteenth century somehow made for a contrasting "warm, protective. . . environment." In the absence of kin, support networks can be (and were) constructed from among unrelated neighbors; surrounded by many kin, most were undoubtedly irrelevant.[7]

One additional point needs to be made: Formal network analysis highlights the division into neighborhoods, precincts, county with which chapter 4 closes and the discussion in chapter 8. In such analysis the density of a social field is an expression of the probability that any two points in the field selected at random are linked by whatever relational variable is being explored. Specifically, density is computed as

$$(A / ((N / 2) * (N - 1))) * 100$$

where N is the number of points in the field and A the number of

---

‖*Source and Notes:* See text for source. Sample sizes by status groups and censuses: (1687) 70, 26, 75, 23, 4; (1704) 77, 55, 86, 25, 3; (1724) 98, 53, 67, 20, 4. The erratic values for the high status group are artifacts of the small samples. Grand means of 7.4 kinship links and 5.6 friendship links are more appropriate.

TABLE 23

Kinship and Friendship among Middlesex
Household Heads by Time

Year	N	Mean Number of Households to Which Linked by:						% Friend Also Kin
		(1)	(2)	(3)	(4)	(5)	(6)	
1687	256	1.1	2.5	0.6	2.1	0.4	3.2	15.2
1704	296	2.0	2.1	1.2	1.3	0.8	3.3	27.4
1724	303	6.2	2.4	4.8	1.1	1.4	7.2	42.9

‖*Source and Note:* See text for description of the sample. Key:
Mean number of households to which linked by (1) kinship, (2) friendship; (3) kinship only; (4) friendship only; (5) kinship and friendship,
(6) kinship and/or friendship.

relationships (or active links) between points.[8] Table 25 demonstrates,
presenting density computations for two arbitrarily selected neighborhoods, one a two-mile circle surrounding Richard Allen and embracing

TABLE 24

The Relationship of Guardians to Their Wards
in Middlesex, 1650–1750

Period	N	Related		Related as				
		Yes	No	(1)	(2)	(3)	(4)	(5)
1650–1689	79	43	36	15	13	10	3	2
		54.4	45.6	34.9	30.2	23.3	7.0	4.7
1690–1709	115	67	48	8	25	20	6	8
		58.3	41.7	11.9	37.3	29.9	9.9	11.9
1710–1750	201	133	68	11	36	66	15	5
		66.2	33.8	8.3	27.1	49.6	11.3	3.8

‖*Source and Notes:* Related as (1) grand or stepparent; (2) sibling
or brother-in-law; (3) aunt or uncle; (4) cousin or other direct relation;
(5) other step-relation. Raw counts are reported in the first row of each
period, percentages in the second—percentage of N in the third and fourth
columns, percentage of all related in the remainder. Stepparents account
for 27.9%, 9.0% and 6.8% of all related guardians for the three periods respectively. The table is based upon the prosopography described in chapter 1.

Allen's circle of friends of the 1680s, the other a similar circle drawn about Elizabeth Montague and embracing her circle of kin in 1704. These are compared to densities for the upper precinct and county computed for friendship networks (1687) and kinship (1704). In every

TABLE 25

Friendship and Kinship Densities
in Middlesex

Level	Density	
	Friendship (1680s)	Kinship (1704)
Neighborhood	42.9	52.0
Precinct	4.3	2.9
County	1.0	0.7

||*Source*: See text.

case the points in the presumed social fields (neighborhood, precinct, county) are household heads. What stands out, of course, is the clustering of friendship and kinship within the neighborhoods and the increasing diffusion of networks as the boundaries of the assumed field are raised, first to the precinct, then county level. In his immediate neighborhood, Allen could call "friend" just about every other household head; while attending services at the Upper Chapel only four out of every hundred chance meetings with a head of household would involve a friend; at county court, only one.

|●|

1. As described in chapter 1.

2. For a description of the original see George A. Collier, "The KINPROGRAM: Accomplishments and Prospects," in Bennett Dyke and Warren T. Morrill, *Genealogical Demography* (New York, 1980), 23–40.

3. Such an assessment of what are termed the content, duration, and direction of a relationship implied by the existence of a documentary link seems necessary when the question at issue is "friendship." Cf. the approach of R. M. Smith, "Kin and Neighbors in a Thirteenth-Century Suffolk Community," *Journal of Family*

History, IV (1979), 219-256.

4. See above, "Population Estimates," and Rutman and Rutman, "'More True and Perfect Lists,'" *Va. Mag. Hist. Biog.*, LXXXVIII (1980), 37-74.

5. The same occurs when the data are broken by the wealth variables as developed below.

6. Reporting *eta* squared computed on native-born (yes or no) as the independent variable and the number of kinship and friendship links as dependent variables, using the entire data set of 855 observations from the three censuses.

7. Daniel Blake Smith, *Inside the Great House*, 176. In a modern study, "typically about nine people [were] named as close" to the respondents, leading the author to conclude that there was "a tendency to limit the number of direct connections formed or maintained at any given time." Muriel Hammer, "Social Access and the Clustering of Personal Connections," *Social Networks*, II (1980), 320, 322.

8. Darrett B. Rutman, "Community Study," *Historical Methods* XIII (1980), 38-39 elaborates upon the procedure.

nine

WEALTH

In recent years the distribution of wealth in an early American community has been largely measured by scrutinizing tax lists (in those circumstances where taxes were assessed on the basis of property) and inventories of personal and occasionally real property made as part of probate. With the exception of tithable lists encompassing but not specifically identifying the servants held by individuals in Lancaster County, which included the area of what would become Middlesex through 1668, nothing approximating the former exists for our county. We do, however, have almost 400 inventories from the years through 1749. We can, to be sure, have confidence in the validity of the appraisals of the various items contained in these inventories and in the total evaluations. They were the judgments of men of the vicinage who knew well the value of things in their society. Indeed, we have for late in our period both inventories and auction records for a series of estates; in three instances the appraised value was 101 percent of the auction value, in one 96 percent.[1] But there are myriad problems associated with the use of inventories.[2]

Unfortunately, ours include only personal property. Some of them are incomplete, giving us only a total evaluation of the property of the deceased but no item-by-item breakdown. Some involve the estates of women. To include them in an analysis would hazard double counting, that is, counting all or part of the wealth of a single family from the vantage point, first, of a deceased husband, then of his widow. In a few instances legal complications required the inventory of the estate of a child. Still other inventories detail Middlesex possessions of individuals who were in actuality residents of other counties, even of England. Some problems were easily resolved by accepting into the analysis only those estates of persons known to be male adult residents of the county at the time of their deaths—346 inventories in all, 335 for which we can establish with precision the age-at-death of the decedent. Still, other problems remain.

In most of the early inventories items are valued in pounds tobacco, but from the turn of the century onward there was a tendency toward stating values in pence, shilling, and pounds, occasionally specified as pounds sterling, more often, by implication if not explicitly, "current money of Virginia." Before analysis of the inventories all values had to be standardized.[3] Values given in the inventories, moreover, reflect the then-current prices for the items listed, but the price level was itself changing from year to year. Again, before analysis, all had to be reduced to one standard level.[4] Finally, inventories are generally assumed to represent a particular segment of the underlying population, one older in the main than the population as a whole. There is, after all, a greater probability of a man dying and hence generating evidence of his wealth (an inventory) at forty or fifty years of age than at twenty. This, together with the assumption that one generally tends to accumulate wealth over the course of a lifetime, leads to the conclusion that inventories overstate the wealth of a community, hence to be useful must be processed in such a way as to give more weight to age-groups presumably underrepresented and less to those presumably overrepresented. Only in this way can the distribution of inventoried wealth be made to approximate the wealth of the real population from which the inventories came.[5] The effects of these last two adjustments on raw data can be seen in figure 21.

The figure depicts the cumulative percent of all inventoried wealth for the period 1720-1750 held by the poorest 10 percent, of the population, the poorest 20 percent, the poorest 30 percent, and so on to the percent held by 100 percent of the population, which would, of course, be 100 percent of the total wealth. The broken

FIGURE 21

Inventory Evaluations of the Personal Property of Deceased
Adult Male Residents of Middlesex, 1720-1750

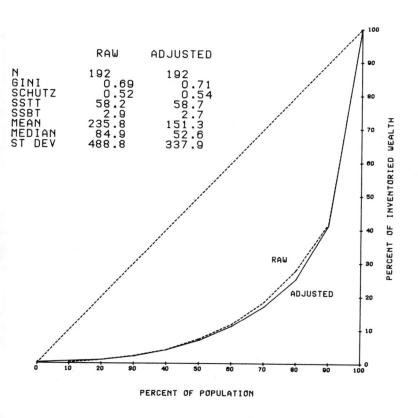

	RAW	ADJUSTED
N	192	192
GINI	0.69	0.71
SCHUTZ	0.52	0.54
SSTT	58.2	58.7
SSBT	2.9	2.7
MEAN	235.8	151.3
MEDIAN	84.9	52.6
ST DEV	488.8	337.9

PERCENT OF POPULATION

||*Source*: See text for a description of the sample and nature of the adjustments.

curve depicts unadjusted or raw inventory values, the solid curve
the data both standardized to a single price level and weighted to
reflect the age structure of the population free, adult, and male.

Figure 21 also displays the tools customarily used for an analysis
of the distribution of wealth. The data are first broken down into

TABLE 26

Decile Breakdown of Adjusted Inventory Evaluations of Personal
Property of Deceased Adult Male Residents
of Middlesex, 1720–1750

Dec-ile	% Total Wealth	Cum %	Mn	Md	SD	Minimum	Maximum
1	0.3	0.3	5.2	5.3	1.3	2.3	7.1
2	0.8	1.1	11.5	11.0	2.6	7.1	15.0
3	1.1	2.2	16.3	16.0	1.2	15.0	19.5
4	1.9	4.1	28.4	28.8	4.8	19.5	36.8
5	2.8	6.9	42.8	40.0	5.8	36.8	52.6
6	4.2	11.1	63.8	65.8	6.4	52.6	77.2
7	5.8	16.9	88.2	85.7	8.4	77.2	102.3
8	8.8	25.8	133.5	143.0	21.3	102.3	169.4
9	15.6	41.3	236.0	209.8	56.6	169.4	358.3
10	58.7	100.0	885.7	583.3	700.7	358.3	3000.0

‖*Source*: See text for a description of the sample [*N* = 192] and the nature of the
adjustments.

deciles—the wealth of the poorest 10 percent, the second poorest 10
percent, and so on through the wealth of the richest 10 percent.
(Table 26 illustrates.) The depiction of the cumulative percentages
of all wealth held by these groups (figure 21) is called a *Lorenz
diagram*, the data lines themselves *Lorenz curves*. If the wealth of
the society is spread absolutely equally among its members—that is,
the lowest 10 percent had 10 percent of the wealth, the lowest 20
percent, 20 percent, and so on—the plot of the cumulative percentages
(the Lorenz curve) would match the diagonal line extending from the
lower left to the upper right, the *line of equality*, as it is called.
Several measures summarize the distribution. *SSTT* is simply the
percent of all wealth held by the top 10 percent—the "size share of
the top ten." In the same way, *SSBT* is the size share (or percent
of the total) held by the bottom one-third of the population. The
Gini index or coefficient is more sophisticated, measuring the size
of the area between the line of equality in the diagram and the line
depicting the real distribution, with a Gini of zero stipulating no
area at all, that the lines are equivalents and the wealth distributed absolutely equally. Absolute inequality—one member of the
population owning all—would produce a Gini of one. The *Schutz
index* or coefficient is a variation of the Gini, measuring the devia-

tion of the slope of the Lorenz curve at its various points from the slope of the line of equality and again ranges from zero (equality) to one (inequality.)[6] All of these measures have an intuitive meaning but they are most useful in making comparisons.[7]

Comparison of the indices when the Middlesex inventories are grouped by the year of death of decedents immediately suggests a series of profound shifts in the diffusion of personal property in the county over time, from a more equal spread of personalty in the seventeenth century to a less equal spread in the first years of the eighteenth, then back toward equality in the years after 1720. (See figure 22.) The shifts could conceivably be more artifacts of the methodology than reflections of reality. Men of great wealth are always few in number in a society and the chance death of two or three in a single period could seriously distort our results. But the movements displayed in an analysis of inventoried wealth are verified in other data.

Figure 23 depicts in the same way the ownership of servants and slaves by male heads-of-household identified in the reconstruction of censuses for three points in time—1668, 1687, and 1724.[8] Again we see a sharp shift from a condition of more to a condition of less equal dispersion, then a gradual movement back toward equality. The figure also affords us a view of the timing of the shift toward inequality (between the censuses of 1668 and 1687) and hints at its cause. Among male household heads of the first census, 39 percent would hold no servants or slaves during their lives, 61 percent would, a relationship reversed by 1687. Of the heads then, 59 per-cent would never hold servants or slaves while 41 percent would. Obviously, the lesser householders were being driven out of the labor market. In part it was a question of blacks—imported in larger and larger numbers during and after the 1680s—involving a greater initial outlay than white servants. But in greater measure it seems a matter of the small holder finding it ever more difficult to work the process described in chapter 3—that is, selling or renting a part of his land to one or two newly freed servants in order to obtain the wherewithal necessary to improve (or obtain servants to work on) the remainder—and of the renter to move eventually into the position of small holder and work the process in turn. For note in figure 24 that the diffusion of land through the society as measured by the highest number of acres owned (or controlled as husband,

FIGURE 22

Adjusted Inventory Evaluations of the Personal Property of Deceased
Adult Male Residents of Middlesex by Date of Death

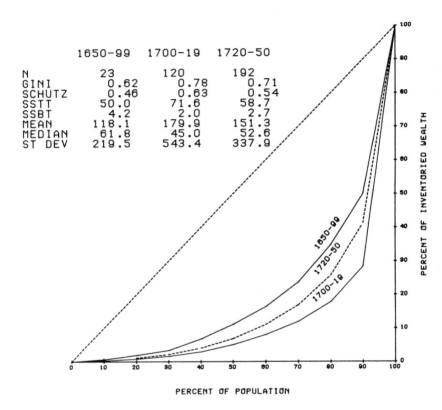

	1650-99	1700-19	1720-50
N	23	120	192
GINI	0.62	0.78	0.71
SCHUTZ	0.46	0.63	0.54
SSTT	50.0	71.6	58.7
SSBT	4.2	2.0	2.7
MEAN	118.1	179.9	151.3
MEDIAN	61.8	45.0	52.6
ST DEV	219.5	543.4	337.9

PERCENT OF POPULATION

||*Source*: See text for a description of the sample and the nature of the adjustments

father, or guardian) by a male head of household during a lifetime,
relatively widespread among the heads of 1668, followed the trend
toward inequality but did *not* rebound. Insofar as labor bulked large
as a key to wealth—in the sense both of generating wealth and being
appraised in the inventories as personal property—the shift in labor

FIGURE 23

Highest Number of Servants and Slaves Held by Male Heads
of Household in Middlesex, 1668, 1687, 1724

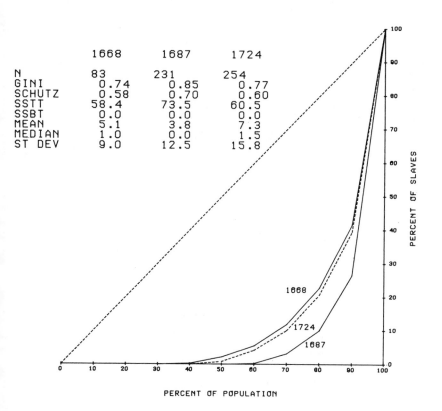

	1668	1687	1724
N	83	231	254
GINI	0.74	0.85	0.77
SCHUTZ	0.58	0.70	0.60
SSTT	58.4	73.5	60.5
SSBT	0.0	0.0	0.0
MEAN	5.1	3.8	7.3
MEDIAN	1.0	0.0	1.5
ST DEV	9.0	12.5	15.8

PERCENT OF SLAVES

PERCENT OF POPULATION

‖*Source:* See text.

among household heads between 1668 and 1687 portended the more
general shift in wealth between the seventeenth and early eighteenth
centuries as measured by the inventories.[9]

The increasing dispersion of laborers (that is to say, slaves) and
of personal property (including slaves) in the eighteenth century is a

FIGURE 24

Highest Number of Acres Controlled in a Lifetime by Male
Heads of Household in Middlesex, 1668, 1687, 1724

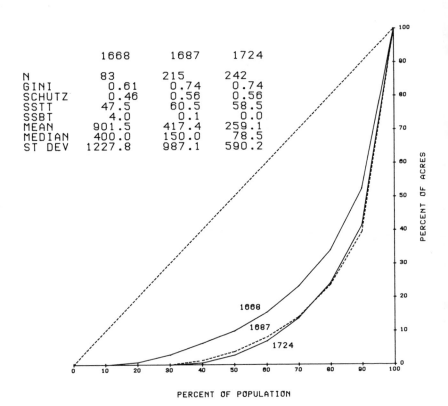

	1668	1687	1724
N	83	215	242
GINI	0.61	0.74	0.74
SCHUTZ	0.46	0.56	0.56
SSTT	47.5	60.5	58.5
SSBT	4.0	0.1	0.0
MEAN	901.5	417.4	259.1
MEDIAN	400.0	150.0	78.5
ST DEV	1227.8	987.1	590.2

Source: See text.

more complicated problem. We discount any supply-side argument
with regard to slaves—that is, the supply of slaves increased, forcing
prices down, hence bringing slaves within the reach of more potential
buyers. Slaves tended to rise in price.[10] Capital accumulation among
small planters and, ultimately, the investment of capital in slave

labor is a possibility, but, as we point out in chapter 6, improbable. The dispersion of slaves among the households by inheritance, and particularly the departure from the county of persons from the lower half of the economic spectrum are also possibilities. The latter would have the effect of removing households with no slaves or few slaves from our analysis, leaving slaves more equally dispersed among the remaining households. And given the relationship between slave holding and the distribution of inventoried wealth, any factor tending to equalize the former would also tend to equalize the latter.

Although the greater diffusion of slaves among Middlesex households was certainly one element in the greater diffusion of wealth indicated in the eighteenth-century inventories, there might well have been another. What we can loosely term the standard of living might have been rising, and with it expectations. Goods and articles which at one point in time were non-existent in the county or exclusively luxury items for the wealthy may well have been diffusing through the society over time, and the very expectation of owning such items might have dropped farther and farther down the economic spectrum. To put the matter simply: Land ownership is not encompassed in the inventories. Let us assume that in the early years a householder put all his efforts into obtaining land and the where-withal to develop it, eschewing pewter plates, chinaware, fine linens, and the like, leaving such items for the rich alone to acquire. Let us further assume that over time—for whatever the reason—householders gave up their quest for ever more land and began acquiring plates and chinaware and linen, eventually coming to expect these accoutrements as a necessary part of life. Notably, both assumptions seem matters of fact in Middlesex. An eighteenth-century shift toward what we can call consumer goods—plates, pots, linens—has been well documented for Maryland. We can see it in Middlesex using the values of beds and bed linens as a surrogate for consumer goods and the inventories of the male heads of house in various reconstructed censuses.[11] The diffusion of such goods through the society over time is illustrated in figure 25. At the same time, however, the mean acreage controlled by heads of household declined—from 417 acres (the mean of the highest number of acres controlled in their lifetimes by male heads-of-house of 1687) to 259 (for those of 1724).[12] Such a shift toward consumer goods would tend to move our indices of equality and inequality toward the equality side. More importantly, it would increase to some extent overall level of wealth in the county as

FIGURE 25

Adjusted Inventory Evaluations of Beds and Bed Linens of
Male Heads of Household, in Middlesex, 1687, 1724

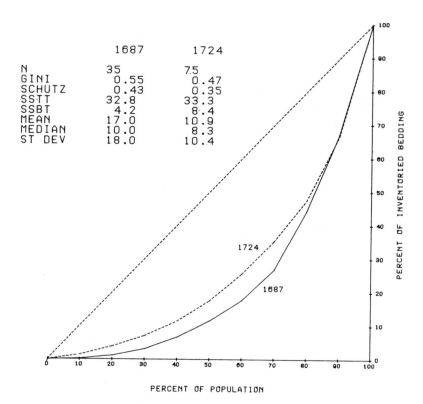

	1687	1724
N	35	75
GINI	0.55	0.47
SCHUTZ	0.43	0.35
SSTT	32.8	33.3
SSBT	4.2	8.4
MEAN	17.0	10.9
MEDIAN	10.0	8.3
ST DEV	18.0	10.4

PERCENT OF POPULATION

reflected in inventories. They do not, recall, include land, hence with individuals putting more in consumer goods and less in land, the inventory totals would become larger.

Decile analysis cannot really speak to such issues. Popular as it is, it has decided drawbacks. It cannot catch changes over time in the overall wealth of a particular community (or differences in overall wealth between communities). Neither can it inform us as to the actual standard of living of the various parts of the community, nor changes in the lifestyle of one part relative to another. For its breakdown into tenths is intrinsically artificial, subsuming in the interest of standardization what might well be groupings more pertinent to (and more natural in) the society and time in question. Indeed, decile analysis is valuable as a tool for comparison largely because it does ignore the particulars of period and place.[13] The artificiality can be seen in table 26. Note that an estate of 7.12*l* is both the maximum of the first decile and the minimum of the second. The same sort of overlapping occurs generally.[14] Note, too, that the minimum value of the highest decile is closer to the mean of the lowest than it is to the mean of its own category. In technical terms, grouping by deciles accounts for relatively little of the variance (or variation) displayed by the data, in this particular case only 56.6 percent.[15]

That deciles do not well reflect the real situation giving rise to the data is generally recognized by scholars, more often than not leading them to offer decile-based indices for comparative purposes, then to re-break the data into what seem intuitively more meaningful groups. An excellent analysis of Maryland inventories for the years 1658 through 1777, for example, grouped them into "poor," "middle," and "rich," defined as 0–50 pounds sterling, 51–225 pounds, and 226 and above.[16] Such grouping is a necessary step, yet more often than not the boundaries of the groups are purely subjective in derivation and, because once set they are applied indiscriminately across time, they effectively mask (as does the decile analysis) potential changes in the gross wealth of the community as a whole and the relative wealth of its parts.

||*Source and Note:* See text for a description of the sample. Values are deflated and adjusted to reflect the age structure of the population of male heads of household of the reconstructed censuses of 1687 and 1724.

What is required in this situation is a procedure which isolates the natural groups within the data stream at different points in time. In other words, we must find that grouping of the data for any particular time which minimizes variation within the groups and maximizes variation between the groups. For example, given a line of data consisting of the values

$$1\ 1\ 1\ 4\ 4\ 4\ 8\ 8\ 8$$

a grouping scheme which broke the data only at four

$$1\ 1\ 1\ 4\ 4\ 4 \qquad 8\ 8\ 8$$

would be far inferior to one that broke it

$$1\ 1\ 1 \qquad 4\ 4\ 4 \qquad 8\ 8\ 8.$$

The former leaves variance within one of the groups; the latter reduces the within-group variance to zero.

TABLE 27

Optimized Groupings of Adjusted Inventory Evaluations of the
Personal Property of Deceased Adult Male Residents
of Middlesex, 1720–1750

Minimum	Maximum	% of N	% Total Wealth	Mn	Md	SD
2.3	73.0	59.7	11.0	27.9	19.5	20.4
77.2	255.1	26.4	23.7	133.5	117.3	48.0
260.9	458.5	7.6	18.3	351.5	360.5	52.7
569.4	637.3	1.6	5.1	605.5	600.0	27.7
821.4	984.7	1.6	8.7	881.9	849.6	53.5
1342.3	1423.5	1.1	11.2	1376.1	1342.3	40.0
1686.0		0.5	4.1	–	–	–
1812.1		0.5	4.4	–	–	–
2581.2		0.5	6.2	–	–	–
3000.0		0.5	7.3	–	–	–

‖*Source and Note*: See text for the sample (N = 192) and the nature of the adjustments, John A. Hartigan, *Clustering Algorithms* (New York, 1975), 81 for the clustering procedure. The last four rows represent single cases.

TABLE 28

Natural Groupings of Adjusted Inventory Evaluations of the
Personal Property of Deceased Adult Male Residents
of Middlesex by Year of Death

Category	Minimum	Maximum	% of N	% Total Wealth	Mn	Md	SD
			THRU	1699			
1	3.8	19.6	31.2	3.6	13.6	15.7	4.8
2	32.7	64.8	28.6	12.8	53.0	51.0	9.2
3	80.8	127.5	13.9	11.1	94.8	89.4	15.7
4	142.5	208.2	20.8	30.9	175.5	177.3	31.5
5	263.9	1309.1	5.6	41.6	872.9	720.9	430.9
			1700 -	1719			
1	1.7	36.1	42.5	3.4	14.4	13.9	8.4
2	37.9	74.8	26.0	7.9	54.6	57.3	11.9
3	77.3	193.2	17.8	12.6	127.0	113.9	37.6
4	200.9	621.2	7.9	14.7	333.0	269.2	150.6
5	1000.0	4974.2	5.8	61.5	1910.4	1131.5	1325.6
			1720 -	1750			
1	2.3	28.8	35.3	3.1	13.1	14.4	6.7
2	29.1	86.1	30.4	11.2	55.5	54.2	17.7
3	88.9	360.5	26.0	31.3	182.2	162.3	82.1
4	368.1	984.7	5.6	21.3	576.0	458.5	204.4
5	1342.3	3000.0	2.7	33.2	1878.3	1686.0	621.9

||*Source and Note*: See text for the source of the sample and the nature of the
adjustments, the text and footnote 17 for the clustering procedures. *N* thru
1699 = 23; 1700-1719 = 120, 1720-1750 = 192.

The techniques of such optimized clustering need not concern us
here. They are both highly technical and dependent on iterative
operations requiring the computer.[17] Table 27 displays the results
of one such optimizing routine applied to the data depicted in figure
21 and table 26, the grouping taking into account 99 percent of the
variation among the inventory values. The ten categories are
obviously cumbersome for our purposes, particularly when the four
highest categories consist simply of the four extreme estates in the
set. We can, however, collapse categories to a manageable number,
allowing the mathematics of natural clustering to guide us in crea-
ting objective groups.[18] When, as in table 28, we do so for the

three periods of figure 21 a number of phenomena come into view.

There was, indeed, an increase in gross wealth (as measured by the inventories) within the county, but it was confined to the upper and middle levels of the society. The boundaries of the lowest economic group (the minimum and maximum) remain relatively constant. Note, moreover, the eighteenth-century decline in the percent of population encompassed by the lowest group and in the measures of central tendency (the mean and median). As one ascends through the categories, however, boundaries and measures of central tendency push upward over time. In sum, the poor of Middlesex were losing ground both in absolute terms and relative to the upper levels of the society, who were amassing ever more. And the "Middling Sort" was growing in both relative size and inventoried wealth.

|●|

1. Middlesex Wills, 1713-1734, 399, 1740-1748, 73, 148-149 and 166-167, 235-239.

2. Gloria L. Main, "The Correction of Biases in Colonial American Probate Records," *Hist. Methods*, VIII (1974), 10-28; her "Probate Records as a Source for Early American History," *WMQ*, 3d Ser., XXXII (1975), 89-99; and Daniel Scott Smith, "Underregistration and Bias in Probate Records: An Analysis of Data from Eighteenth-Century Hingham, Massachusetts," ibid., 100-110 are already near-classic statements of the problems as they apply to early American history.

3. Our way has been to convert tobacco to current money by applying the price series depicted in table 1, and sterling to current using factors of 1.2155 (through 1728) and 1.25 (from 1729).

4. We have applied a Maryland price series (1700 = 100) developed by P. M. G. Harris and reported in Clemens, *Atlantic Economy*, 228. The use of composite annual factors drawn from Maryland might seem unduly hazardous but even more hazardous would be to attempt to establish deflators from the limited materials of a single county. Harris is currently develping a far more powerful and sophisticated set of deflators on the basis of prices from throughout the Chesapeake region. When available for general use they will allow a more extensive analysis than that attempted here. In any event, deflation on the basis of Harris's published series had minimal effect, by itself shifting the Gini index from 0.692 (raw) to 0.686 and the SSTT from 58.2 to 57.5.

5. We have adjusted the inventories to the age profile of the free, adult, male population of the reconstructed census nearest in point of time to the greatest number of inventories being used for a period. (On the censuses see Rutman and Rutman, "'More True and Perfect Lists,'" *Va. Mag. Hist. Biog.*, LXXXVIII [1980], 37-54.) Thus in analyzing the inventories of 1650-1699 we have adjusted to the age profile (free, male, age greater than or equal to 20) of 1687, 1700-1719 to

that of 1704, and 1720-1750 to 1724. An additional corrective is sometimes made to rectify a bias presumed to exist between probated and unprobated estates. But in the absence of evidence as to the direction and extent of the bias, the correction tends to be "the time honored one of the educated guess"—quoting Carole Shammas, "Constructing a Wealth Distribution from Probate Records," *Journ. Int. Hist.* IX (1978), 298. Aside from our being uncomfortable with such guesswork, we did not feel the correction necessary given our primary objective—viz., trends rather than precise numbers—and a research strategy involving both probate and non-probate materials. Note infra the similar results.

6. In general see Joseph E. Stiglitz, "Distribution of Income and Wealth among Individuals," *Econometrica*, XXXVII (1969), 382-397, and Anthony B. Atkinson, "On the Measurement of Inequality," *Journal of Economic Theory*, II (1970), 244-263. For computations see Charles M. Dollar and Richard J. Jensen, *Historian's Guide to Statistics: Quantitative Analysis and Historical Research* (New York, 1971), 122-125, and Robert R. Schutz, "On the Measurement of Income Inequality," *American Economic Review*, XLI (1951), 107-122. All computations were done on a point basis rather than groups using a variation of the routine described in James P. Whittenburg and Randall G. Pemberton, "Measuring Inequality: A Fortran Program for the Gent [sic] Index, Schutz Coefficient, and Lorenz Curve," *Hist. Methods*, X (1977), 77-84.

7. Unfortunately, intuition generally starts with the notion that absolute equality is an absolute good, therefore the closer a Gini or Schutz coefficient is to zero the better. This is unrealistic. Alice Hanson Jones, *Wealth of a Nation to Be: The American Colonies on the Eve of the Revolution* (New York, 1980), 259-290, and Gloria L. Main, "Inequality in Early America: The Evidence from Probate Records of Massachusetts and Maryland," *Journ. Int. Hist.*, VII (1977), 559-581, offer some benchmarks to aid our intuition in the present instance. Gini indices for Maryland, 1675-1719, calculated for successive five-year periods, fluctuated between 0.6 and 0.68 through 1709, then moved to 0.74. Ginis calculated for the same period for rural Suffolk County, Massachusetts fluctuated between 0.44 and 0.53. In estimating total physical wealth in the American colonies in 1774 among free wealthholders, Jones calculated a Gini of 0.66; by region: the South, 0.68, the Middle Colonies, 0.54, New England, 0.61. A Gini for English income, 1688, has been calculated at 0.61 with Jones estimating well above 0.66 for wealth, perhaps even above 0.73. A Gini for land ownership in England, 1873, has been calculated at 0.82 when cottagers are excluded, 0.93 when included. The Gini coefficient for the distribution of wealth in the United States, 1962, has been calculated at 0.76.

8. Rutman and Rutman, "'More True and Perfect Lists,'" *Va. Mag. Hist. Biog.*, LXXXVIII (1980), 37-54. Specifically, we are using here the highest number of servants or slaves owned (or controlled as husband, father, guardian) by a head in any year of his lifetime. We use these three particular censuses because they highlight the shift. Results based on other censuses conform.

9. In the main the heads of 1687 would die after 1699, hence those whose inventories we have would largely fall in the middle period, 1700-1719. Sample sizes (the number of census-generated heads) differ between figures 23 and 24 because of missing data. There were instances in which we knew a head owned or controlled land and/or labor but we could not estimate how much with any degree of reliability. In such instances we dropped the head from the particular analysis.

10. Russell R. Menard, "From Servants to Slaves: The Transformation of the Chesapeake Labor System," *South. Stud.*, XVI (1977), 372, Clemens,

Atlantic Economy, 61–62, 154, 166.

11. Lois Green Carr and Lorena S. Walsh, "Inventories and the Analysis of Wealth and Consumption Patterns in St. Mary's County, Maryland, 1658–1777," *Hist. Methods*, XII (1980), 81–104.

12. See figure 24.

13. And it is popular, we suggest, only because of the paramountcy of questions of equality and inequality in the minds of investigators.

14. The overlapping is exaggerated by the method of weighting required to adjust for age, one accomplished by reproducing cases in much the same way as that described as the "alternative procedure" in Norman H. Nie, et al., *SPSS: Statistical Package for the Social Sciences* (2d edn., New York, 1975), 130–131. But such overlapping is a common phenomenon in decile breakdowns of raw data as well, occurring whenever a decile boundary lands between two similar values.

15. Reporting *eta*-squared converted to a percentage.

16. Carr and Walsh, "Consumption Patterns," *Hist. Methods*, XIII (1980), 91 is but one of many examples. Russell R. Menard, P. M. G. Harris, and Lois Green Carr, "Opportunity and Inequality: The Distribution of Wealth on the Lower Western Shore of Maryland, 1638–1705," *Md. Hist. Mag.*, LXIX (1974), 180, using in part the same data, use a quite different set of breakpoints.

17. On clustering in general see Brian Everitt, *Cluster Analysis* (London, 1974), Michael R. Anderberg, *Cluster Analysis for Applications* (New York, 1973), and Charles Wetherell, "A Note on Hierarchical Clustering," *Hist. Methods*, X (1977), 109–116. We used an improved leader procedure based upon John A. Hartigan, *Clustering Algorithms* (New York, 1975), 81. In this algorithm the data are broken, first, on the basis of the mean and the case farthest from the mean as leaders, with all other cases being assigned to one or the other according to distance, then successively entering as a new leader the case farthest from its particular leader. The algorithm produces a tight fit but tends to isolate extreme values as groups unto themselves (as in table 27).

18. In collapsing categories we were guided by our own variant of the improved leader procedure, viz., entering the data with the mean as a leader to form an initial cluster the mean of which is the most variant of all possible cluster means from the existing leader; this initial cluster is then separated and what remains of the data is reentered with its mean as leader to form still another cluster, the mean of which is again most distant, continuing the process until the requisite number of groups is formed. Collapsing categories obviously reduces the fit of the categorization to the data, in the case of the 1720–1750 inventories from the 99% fit of table 27 (*eta*-squared transformed to a percentage) to 89% for the 1720–1750 portion of table 28. By way of contrast, the subjective categorization used by Carr and Walsh (note 16) applied to this same data accounted for only 47% of the variance.

highest number of servants or slaves which we can associate with
the individual. In what follows we will refer to these three as
simply "estate," "land," and "labor." We know also whether what is
termed a "social honorific" was ever applied to an individual: Was
a man ever referred to as "Mister Jones," "Sir John," "John Jones,
Gentleman," or "John Jones, Esquire"? Was a woman called "Lady
Ann"? If so, we have recorded the highest honorific known to have
been accorded.[3] From militia lists and the like we have knowledge of
military rank and can establish the highest rank known to have been
achieved by an individual. We frequently know an individual's occupation. Most often it was simply "planter," but sometimes we know of
a craft or profession being conducted on the side and the individual
becomes for us a "planter and tailor" or "planter and lawyer." Occasionally, particularly toward the end of the period, an individual
appeared as a pure specialist; in his shop in Urbanna he was solely
a "tailor."[4] Finally, we know the offices an individual held—"petit
juror," "highway surveyor," "churchwarden," "county court justice,"
"councillor," and the like. More often than not these are considered
by historians in the context of power, but for reasons outlined in
chapter 5 we begin by associating them simply with status.

All but two of our variables—military rank and offices—apply
equally to men and women. In practice, however, our data confine
us at the outset to males. There are few instances of women with
estates, land, labor, honorifics, even fewer in which we know an
occupation, and then it is usually one taken up by a widow in
straitened circumstances—Dorothy Needles brewing beer and cider in
her widowhood comes to mind.[5] We are, moreover, limited to males
meeting particular criteria. All of our variables pertain to adults,
therefore children, even male children, must be excluded. And we must
allow individuals time to make their mark, hence exclude those who
died or left the county (and our view) after only a few years of adult-
hood. When these considerations are applied to our data we arrive at
1,653 cases: Males whose year of birth we know or can estimate on
reasonable grounds, who lived to age twenty-one, and who remained
under our observation for at least six years thereafter.[6] The six years
are, of course, a purely arbitrary number. Conceivably we are allowing
nowhere near enough time for an individual to establish himself. To
test for such a possibility we need still another piece of information,
an eighth variable: the age at which the individual died or left the
county. For convenience we will call it simply "age out."

TABLE 29

Social Honorifics and Wealth Variables
in Middlesex, 1650–1750

Honorific	Wealth Variables							
	Estate			Land			Labor	
	N	Mn	SD	*N*	Mn	SD	Mn	SD
None	227	91	113	1405	90	229	1	3
Mister	61	448	697	211	729	1133	9	14
Gentleman	9	1354	1542	32	1359	1186	30	36
Esquire	2	3193	1141	5	3139	1775	70	48

‖*Source and Notes*: See text for the derivation of the sample and definitions of the variables. The second *N* applies to both land and labor. 41% of the variation in estates, 29% in land, and 37% in labor is subsumed in the honorific categories (reporting *eta* squared converted to a percentage).

A technical point: Seven of the variables mentioned (estate, land, labor, age out, honorifics, military rank, and occupation) are measurements, but measurements of different sorts. The first three are of the most complete type—*ratio*. Land, for example, is a measure of an exact amount, hence we can know an exact difference between cases. A man with 200 acres is separated by exactly 50 acres from a man with 150. And the absence of any land at all is measured by a zero. Age out is an *interval* measurement, on a par with the first three in everything except the meaning of zero; it does not imply the absence of the thing being measured. Military rank and honorifics, however, are of a definitely lesser type of measurement. They are *ordinals* in that they reflect only the order of something. Military rank is an ordinal by definition. On the scale denoted by rank, a "captain" is something greater than a "corporal" and a "colonel" something more than a "captain," but exactly how much of what it is that military rank denotes separates these three points is unknown. Social honorifics are, initially, only intuitively ordinal. In the abstract there is no reason beyond the historian's intuition— admittedly born of a great deal of reading of both the documents from and literature about the period—to think that an "esquire" ranks above a "gentleman" who ranks above a "mister" who ranks above a person accorded no honorific at all. But

TABLE 30

Military Rank and Office Holding in Middlesex,
1650–1750

Highest Military Rank Achieved	Highest Office Achieved															
	1	2	3	4	5	6	7	8	9	10	11	12	13	14	15	16
Musician	1			1												
Corporal	2		3	2		2	6									
Sergeant	1		2		1		1									
Cornet									1		1					
Lieutenant	1		1													
Captain	2	1		1			3	2		1	5		4	3		1
Major								1						2		
Lieut Col											1					1
Colonel	2											1	2	3	1	6
Maj Gen																1

‖*Source and Notes*: See text for source. The numbers represent frequencies, e.g., 6 Corporals achieved office #7 as a Highest Office. Key to "Highest Office": (1) None, (2) Petit Juror, (3) Appraiser of Estates, (4) Processioner, (5) Clerk (Vestry); (6) Constable, (7) Surveyor of Highways, (8) Auditor of Accounts, (9) Warehouse Officer, (10) Churchwarden, (11) Justice, (12) Coroner, (13) Sheriff, (14) Burgess, (15) Port Collector, (16) Councillor.

intuition gains credence when we sense the power of the ordinal scale to organize other data, as in table 29.

Finally, occupation is of the lowest sort of measurement: *nominal*. It does nothing but denominate a case to be of one particular kind to the exclusion of all other kinds in the list. A man is a "tailor," hence not a "lawyer" or "brewer" or even (given our coding) a "planter–tailor." No scaling is implied by a nominal, no sense of there being any particuar order or distance between one occupation and another.

What of our other variable, offices? In raw form this is not even a measurement, only a bit of information: A man held a particular office at a particular point in time, perhaps holding other office at the same time and probably a good many offices over the course of a lifetime. We can, however, create an ordinal from these bits. Our way has been to look at all of the offices held by Middlesex men and arrange them into an order in part on an intuitive basis,[7] in part by considering the derivation of authority associated with the office,[8] and in part by the size of the geographic jurisdiction involved.[9] With a rank order of offices in hand, the data were processed to generate from the variable "offices" a new ordinal variable: the highest office known to have been held by an individual.

The excursion into types or levels of measurement has been a necessary prelude. We reason that our seven basic variables— omitting for the moment age out—have something to do with status in

TABLE 31

Measure of Association among Status
Variables in Middlesex

	AO	Est	Acr	Lbr	Hnr	MR	HO	Occ
AO	–	299	1653	1653	1653	69	1653	1171
Est	.12 r	–	299	299	299	30	299	291
Acr	.18 r	.64 r	–	1653	1653	69	1653	1171
Lbr	.25 r	.75 r	.61 r	–	1653	69	1653	1171
Hnr	.20 e .19 r	.64 e .58 r	.54 e .53 r	.61 e .56 r	–	69	1653	1171
MR	.34 e .05 r	.65 e .55 r	.82 e .63 r	.60 e .53 r	.81 g	–	69	68
HO	.45 e .35 r	.70 e .50 r	.71 e .54 r	.69 e .51 r	.83 g	.64 g	–	1171
Occ	.30 e .18 r	.62 e .12 r	.52 e .17 r	.55 e .15 r	.20 l	.31 l	.10 l	–

‖*Source and Notes*: See text for the derivation of the sample. Sample sizes are entered above the diagonal, coefficients below. Coefficients are italicized when insignificant at the .01 level. Key to variables (further defined in the text): AO = Age Out; Est = Estate; Acr = Acres; Lbr = Labor; Hnr = Honorific; MR = Military Rank; HO = Highest Office; Occ = Occupation. Key to coefficients: r = Pearsonian Product Moment Coefficient; e = *eta*, g = *gamma*, l = *lambda*.

Middlesex. Some, the wealth variables and occupation, conceivably generated status. Honorifics to some extent at least reflected the status accorded individuals by the community. Military rank and highest office achieved perhaps did a little of both. A man might have achieved high office or rank in part because of status and gained greater status by virtue of the achievement. Ideally all seven, and only these seven, were directly and inviolately related to status and therefore to each other. All men achieving the same status left the same size estate, had the same number of acres and laborers, and the same highest office and military rank, the same occupation, and all were referred to by the same honorific. In such an ideal situation we need only know the value of one of the variables to know all of the others and the individual's status. The opposite of the ideal is that the seven were absolutely unrelated, that the size of an estate, military rank, and the like were random attributes—gifts from a promiscuous god, so to speak. The fact lies somewhere between the two and is susceptible to estimation by one of several statistical techniques, exactly which depending largely upon the level of measurement involved. Table 30 illustrates—a tabulation of military rank and highest office. Both scales are ordinal, and we have chosen *gamma* as an appropriate measure of the relationship between the two.[10] Like all measures we will be using, *gamma* is free to run from zero (absolutely no relationship) to one (an inviolate relationship).[11] From the tabulation we compute a *gamma* of 0.64, indicative of a probability that in 64 out of 100 instances in which we know the rank of an individual on one scale we can correctly state his rank on the other. In the way of such things, 0.64 is evidence of a moderately strong relationship.

What can be done with one pair of our variables can be done with all, giving the results presented in the lower half of the matrix depicted in table 31. The indices of association reported differ according to the types of measurement involved. And the intuitive meanings of the indices differ. *Gamma*, as we said, can be construed as a probability of correct prediction; *eta* and *r*, when squared, infer the proportion of the variation in one variable accounted for or "explained" by the other, *r* assuming a linear relationship, *eta* making no such assumption. Note in this regard the failure of age out to account for much of anything; confining our sample to men in observation for at least six of their adult years seems to have done an adequate job. But the major point in the table is the fact that moderately strong to strong relationships prevail among our seven basic

TABLE 32

Relative Discriminating Power of Status and
Wealth Variables in Middlesex

Step	Variable	Standardized Canonical Discriminant Function Coefficients		
		1	2	3
1	Highest Office	0.96	−0.39	0.08
2	Highest Honorific	0.58	0.45	−0.74
3	Land	0.10	0.46	0.47
4	Labor	−0.11	0.41	0.45
5	Age Out	−0.02	−0.25	0.06
	Eigenvalue	11.58	0.46	0.08
	Percent of Variance Subsumed	95.52	3.79	0.68
	Canonical Correlation	0.96	0.56	0.28

‖*Source and Notes:* See text for the derivation of the sample and
definition of the variables and measures. The analysis was undertaken
using the Discriminant subprogram available in the Statistical Package for
the Social Sciences (DECsystem-10, Version M, Release 8.1) described in
Norman H. Nie, et al., *SPSS: Statistical Package for the Social
Sciences* (2nd Edn.: New York, 1970), 434–467. Rao's *V* was used as the
step criterion and the analysis was constrained by the group properties
of the initial classification described in the text. A fourth function
is omitted as of negligible effect.

variables, hinting more at an ordered world than at a promiscuous
god; that what we can term wealth variables (estate, land, labor) are
well linked to variables more overtly status-oriented (honorifics,
military rank, office); and that among the latter, highest office
achieved stands out for its strong relationships across the board.

The power of highest office to organize the data shows itself clearly in a more strenuous (and statistically esoteric) analysis which has as its goal the best possible division into groups of a number of cases described by particular variables. Again, the mathematics of the technique need not concern us. They are analogous to our finding natural wealth groups by minimizing within-group variance in the section on wealth.[12] Suffice it to say that in defining functions by which we effect an optimal grouping of our sample, the analysis consistently underscored the organizing power of highest office achieved.[13] Table 32 depicts the results of one such attempt using the five variables highest office, honorifics, land, labor, and age out.[14] "Step" in the table denotes the order in which each variable was drawn into the analysis, the order in turn being based upon the discriminating power of the variable. The coefficients inform us as to the relative importance of each variable in defining a given function. And the eigenvalues, percents of variance subsumed, and canonical correlations are measures of the relative importance of each function in discriminating groups within the data. In sum, the table tells us that the first function generated was dominated by highest office achieved and honorifics, and that this first was by far the most important function in defining the groups.

Table 32, with its "eigenvalues" and "canonical correlations," is offered for the most part for those who are at home with such things and can legitimately expect the wherewithal to make a technical judgment of our findings. Those findings, however, can be stated in another and simpler way.

Consider two classifications of the data—the 1,653 Middlesex men described by our eight variables: In the first classification, each individual within the sample was assigned to one of five groups on the basis only of highest office achieved, honorific, and (where we had information) highest achieved military rank. We conceive of these five groups as status groups:

> Low Status
> Low Middle Status
> Middle Status
> High Middle Status
> High Status

Intuition and the results of preliminary analysis—the correlation matrix depicted in table 31, for example—guided us in formulating the rules for assignment to one group or another. These rules are outlined in table 33. Highest office achieved gave us an initial assignment, corrected (if *upward* correction was warranted) by military rank and honorifics. Thus an individual whose highest office was that of appraiser of estates was assigned to the "low middle" group. If the individual was known to have achieved a militia sergeancy, he was upgraded to "middle." And if he was referred to at some point in time as "gentleman" he was upgraded again, to the "high middle" group.

The second classification utilized the functions derived in the discriminant analysis reported in table 32. Again, status assignments were made on a scale of "low" to "high." But this time all of the variables listed were utilized. In effect, the wealth variables, ignored in the first classification, were entered in the second. Once completed, the two classifications were compared. In 94 percent of the cases the assignment of status was the same. Moreover, when each of the ninety-seven instances in which the two classifications differed was reviewed in the light of *all* of our knowledge of the individuals involved—a breadth of knowledge far exceeding what could be entered into the purely quantitative analysis—good and sufficient reasons for each difference could be discerned.

William Beaumont is a case in point. Assigned initially—that is, by the rules of table 33—as a man of low middle status, Beaumont was elevated to middle status by the second classification. Yet while Beaumont had arrived in the county in 1681 as heir to a grandfather's 800 acres and seems to have been highly regarded at first (within seven years he was named a surveyor of highways), he lost half his land within a few years of that appointment, for the last twelve years of his life served only as a juror and grand juror, and died leaving an estate of but ninety-one pounds. Given these circumstances, the initial assignment seems a more accurate generalization of the way in which the county looked upon him.

Jacob Stiff is another. Again, our initial assignment was low middle, but in this instance the more complex classification downgraded him to low. Stiff was a native son who was called upon constantly to undertake public service. At age twenty-five he was named a constable but asked to be excused on the grounds of illiteracy. He continued to serve in public offices of lower rank, however, came to own or control some 900 acres of land, and either learned to read or was considered so able that he did not need to, for in 1718 and again

Status

TABLE 33

Rules for Status Assignments

Status	Highest Office Achieved	Highest Military Rank Achieved	Highest Honorific Accorded
Low	None Sexton		
Low Middle	Grand Juror Grand Jury Foreman Petit Juror Petit Jury Foreman Appraiser of Work or Labor Appraiser of Estates Patroller Tobacco Counter Processioner		
Middle	Reader Clerk (Vestry) Constable Bailiff Undersheriff Surveyor of Highways Deputy Clerk (Court) Levy Collector Auditor of Accounts Viewer of Leather Tobacco Warehouse Officer	Musician Corporal Sergeant Ensign	Mister
High Middle	King's Attorney Clerk (Court) Vestryman (& Minister) Churchwarden Justice Coroner Sheriff Burgess	Cornet Lieutenant Captain Major Lieutenant Colonel Colonel	Gentleman
High	Port Collector Trustee (William & Mary) Surveyor General Attorney General Treasurer Receiver General Auditor General Clerk (Burgesses) Secretary of State Councillor President of Council Deputy Governor	Major General	Esquire

in 1723 he was named (and served as) a constable. As with Beaumont, the initial classification seems to mirror more adequately his position in the community.

One final example. Our initial classification set William Stanard as a man of low middle status, the second raised him to a place in the middle group. Stanard arrived in the county around 1677 and

TABLE 34

Status and Wealth in Middlesex,
1650–1750

Status	*N*	Mn	Md	SD
L A N D				
Low	986	35.2	0.0	156.8
Low Middle	234	171.7	100.0	282.5
Middle	290	307.6	200.1	371.8
High Middle	126	978.8	635.5	1115.9
High	17	3027.1	2250.0	2246.6
L A B O R				
Low	986	0.3	0.0	1.2
Low Middle	234	1.9	0.0	3.6
Middle	290	4.0	1.4	6.3
High Middle	126	16.5	8.3	20.6
High	17	47.7	34.0	44.1
E S T A T E				
Low	95	44.0	25.3	50.3
Low Middle	62	91.4	59.5	99.2
Middle	103	174.4	112.0	311.1
High Middle	35	801.5	580.0	917.2
High	4	2662.5	3193.0	2246.6

‖*Source:* See text.

married Henry Thacker's widow, Eltonhead Connoway. Thacker was a man of high middle status, his wife among the best-connected women in the county. Esteem accrued to Stanard by virtue of the marriage (and the property he controlled as a result). In 1679 he was named a surveyor of highways and might well have made the court or vestry eventually. But there were apparently early suspicions as to his

TABLE 35

Career Paths among Middlesex Officeholders,
1680–1750

Office	*N*	Percent of Holders Serving Earlier as:							
		PJ	EA	GJ	C	SH	V	J	Sh
PJ	314	–	17.8	14.3	7.0	8.9	0.3	0.6	0.0
EA	326	41.1	–	22.7	10.7	11.0	1.2	1.5	0.0
GJ	203	51.7	31.0	–	13.8	13.8	0.5	0.0	0.0
C	84	53.6	26.2	27.4	–	15.5	0.0	0.0	0.0
SH	130	60.0	45.4	41.5	23.1	–	3.8	3.8	0.0
V	30	60.0	20.0	53.3	16.7	26.7	–	26.7	13.3
J	32	62.5	28.1	56.3	18.8	31.3	31.3	–	0.0
Sh	16	75.0	62.5	37.5	31.3	56.3	62.5	100.0	–

||*Source and Note*: The table is based upon 1,135 entries into
various offices in Middlesex by individuals (1) whose year of
birth we knew or could reasonably estimate, (2) who lived to at
least age 21 and remained under observation for at least six years
thereafter, (3) who entered public office in the county after 1679,
and (4) who began their public service in the county in an office
other than one listed on table 33 as carrying "High Middle" or
"High" status connotation. Key to offices: PJ = Petit Juror,
EA = Estate Appraiser, GJ = Grand Juror, C = Constable,
SH = Surveyor of Highways, V = Vestryman, J = Justice, Sh = Sheriff.

intentions or abilities in handling the Thacker estate and in 1681 the
court set about restricting his control to protect the interests of the
Thacker orphans. By 1686 Stanard had abandoned the county, his
debts, his wife, and his family.

The conclusion from such examples seems inescapable. The initial
classification, based largely on the highest office achieved, was a
better reflection of the reality in Middlesex than the second, in which
wealth variables entered the classifying scheme. Wealth counted, to be
sure. The correlations of table 31 and the summary statistics of
table 34 indicate as much. But within limits there was opportunity
for men to win or lose the esteem of their neighbors—status—apart
from wealth.

The ability to isolate what we have referred to as status groups
underlies much of the structure of chapter 5. What follows speaks to
detail offered there and elsewhere in the primary volume of this work.
Table 35 suggests the typical (but not inviolate) career paths followed

by the men of Middlesex—the phenomenon of men beginning their public service as petit jurors and estate appraisers and rising, if they rose at all, through grand jury service, terms as constable or surveyors of highway, finally achieving a seat on the court or vestry. Record lapses (the absence of jury lists for the early county, for example) required the exclusion from the table of those who began public service in the county before 1680. The tabulation also excludes those whose public service in the county began in an office connoting high or high middle status in recognition of the fact that men of exceptionally high intrinsic status—Wormeleys, Chicheleys, and the like— served no apprenticeship in public office.

TABLE 36

Mean Age on Entering Selected Offices in Middlesex, 1680–1750

(A)		(B)	
Office	Age	Office	Age
Petit Juror	30.2	Estate Appraiser	32.9
Constable	29.7	Surveyor Highways	32.8
Justice	33.1	Sheriff	37.5
		Processioner	37.6
		Tobacco Counter	40.8

‖*Source and Notes*: The table is based upon the sample described in table 35. Offices presumed to encompass less immediate and less direct involvement in decisions regarding property are grouped under (A), those presumed to involve more under (B). The mean ages of processioners and tobacco counters are based on samples of 7 and 31 respectively.

The rationality of the social processes at work shows again in table 36, a depiction of the mean age on entering particular offices with positions of roughly equal rank divided between those in which the incumbent was more or less immediately and directly involved in decisions relative to property. We have added to the former (more directly involved) two additional positions: processioners and tobacco counters. Although relatively lowly positions in some respects, both were obviously considered by the society as requiring exceptional

TABLE 37

Mean Age of Middlesex Men on Entering Public Office
and Achieving Their Highest Level of Office
by Father's Status, 1680–1750

Father's Status	Level of Son's Highest Office				All
	2	3	4	5	
	AGE ON ENTERING OFFICE				
Low	33.4	27.3	-	-	32.9
	36	*3*	*0*	*0*	*39*
Low Middle	29.4	28.5	-	-	29.3
	45	*4*	*0*	*0*	*49*
Middle	29.2	25.7	-	-	28.8
	86	*12*	*0*	*0*	*98*
High Middle	26.6	26.1	23.2	-	26.1
	51	*10*	*9*	*0*	*70*
High	22.5	28.0	22.4	-	22.9
	2	*1*	*8*	*0*	*11*
	ON ACHIEVING HIGHEST LEVEL				
Low	37.1	32.9	40.0	-	35.4
	21	*17*	*1*	*0*	*39*
Low Middle	31.6	27.0	-	--	30.4
	36	*13*	*0*	*0*	*49*
Middle	31.6	32.0	36.1	--	32.0
	59	*32*	*7*	*0*	*98*
High Middle	31.5	28.1	30.2	29.7	30.1
	26	*21*	*20*	*3*	*70*
High	-	--	24.4	33.5	27.7
	0	*0*	*7*	*4*	*11*

‖*Source and Notes*: The table is based upon the sample described in table 35.
enlarged by removing the fourth restriction, but diminished by adding as a
requirement the necessity of knowing the father's status. The levels of office
are those depicted in table 33. Sample sizes are given in italics in the second
row of each category.

maturity and experience. Almost three quarters of all tobacco counters had served earlier as petit jurors, the same proportion as estate appraisers, over half as grand jurors and surveyors of highways, a third as constables; 43 percent of the processioners had served earlier as petit jurors, 39 percent as grand jurors, 36 percent as estate appraisers, 23 percent as surveyors of highways, and 17 percent as constables.[15] It might be argued that the very task allotted to the processioners required great age. They were, after all, repositories of the collective memory of metes and bounds. But the argument does not necessarily apply to the degree of experience in public service apparently required, and it does not at all apply to the maturity and experience required of tobacco counters. For positions in which the individual so directly and personally decided matters of property—land, tobacco—the society obviously required status of a particular kind. We cannot help but feel that had William Provert lived he would ultimately have served as a processioner, tobacco counter, or both.[16]

Table 37 speaks more generally to the issue of the age at which men began public service and achieved their highest status. If, as we argue, officeholding is a strong reflection of a man's status in the society and at the same time there is a specific path of officeholding which is to be followed, the age at which a man entered various offices will reflect the accrual of status to him through life. Unfortunately, our data preclude our applying the logic in pristine fashion. The offices of table 35 merely suggest a career ladder; they do not delineate clear rungs. We must, consequently, deal in terms of levels of office commensurate with what we think of as status levels, resorting again to the rules of asignment sketched earlier (table 33). And rather than track men as they climbed the ladder, we can only ask at what age they began the climb, and at what age they achieved their highest office (status). The upper portion of table 37 addresses the first, but also tests for the effect of the father's status upon the entry point of the son.[17] These two are clearly related. Sons of fathers of higher status tended to begin public service at a higher level and younger age than sons of fathers of lower status. The lower part of the table addresses the second question, again testing for the effect of the father's status. When the tables are broken down by the period men first entered public service another phenomenon comes into view. Across time, the relative situations of sons of fathers of various statuses remained the same, but all—and particularly those of lower

TABLE 38

Mean Age of Middlesex Men on Entering Public Office
and Achieving Their Highest Level of Office
by Father's Status and Time

Father's Status	Sons Maturing		
	1680–1699	1700–1719	1720–1750
A G E O N E N T E R I N G O F F I C E			
Low	27.5	31.3	36.7
	6	*17*	*16*
Low Middle	28.0	25.6	31.5
	5	*15*	*29*
Middle	25.0	26.9	31.4
	10	*43*	*45*
High Middle	24.9	25.1	28.5
	22	*26*	*22*
High	24.0	22.0	22.8
	3	*3*	*5*
O N A C H I E V I N G H I G H E S T L E V E L			
Low	31.8	34.8	37.4
	6	*17*	*16*
Low Middle	30.0	27.3	32.1
	5	*15*	*29*
Middle	31.0	31.7	32.6
	10	*43*	*45*
High Middle	30.1	29.8	30.3
	22	*26*	*22*
High	25.0	30.0	28.0
	3	*3*	*5*

‖*Source and Notes*: See table 37.

ranked fathers—tended to begin public service and achieve their
highest level at a later age. (Table 38.)

Fathers clearly gave sons a boost on the ladder toward status
in Middlesex. Table 37 indicates as much. So, too, does table 39.

TABLE 39

Interaction of Status between Fathers and
Sons in Middlesex, 1650-1750

Father's Status	Son's Status				
	Low	Low Middle	Middle	High Middle	High
DATA					
Low	97	20	19	1	1
Low Middle	59	35	15	1	0
Middle	101	55	35	11	0
High Middle	24	21	30	28	3
High	1	0	2	8	4
INTERACTION INDICES					
Low	24.9	-6.1	6.2	-84.9	-33.6
Low Middle	13.0	26.4	5.9	-81.1	-100.0
Middle	5.1	12.4	8.3	-3.5	-100.0
High Middle	-74.5	49.1	0.5	29.7	0.7
High	-97.4	-100.0	-83.6	12.7	57.7
MODEL					
Low	44.3	4.7	-42.7	-70.3	-82.7
Low Middle	4.6	25.7	-2.0	-49.2	-70.3
Middle	-42.8	-2.0	22.3	-2.0	-42.7
High Middle	-70.4	-49.3	-2.0	25.7	4.7
High	-82.4	-70.4	-42.8	4.6	44.3

‖*Source*: The table is based on the sample described in table 37
enlarged by removing the restriction to individuals entering public
office in Middlesex after 1679. See text and footnote 18 for definitions.

Here we have again assigned fathers and sons to particular categories
of status, using the rules outlined in table 33. We then asked: In what
category did sons fall relative to fathers? The uppermost segment of
table 39 offers an answer. Of 138 sons of low status fathers in the
sample we are using, 97 (70 percent) achieved for themselves nothing
more than low status; of 15 sons of high status fathers, eight (53
percent) achieved high middle status, four (27 percent) achieved high
status. We can go a step further in isolating the interaction of fathers'
status and sons' by converting the actual numbers into what we will
refer to as "interaction indices"—the middle segment of table 39.[18]

The meaning of the indices comes clear when we explore what might be expected under certain conditions. If, for example, there were complete and absolute independence between the status of fathers and that achieved by sons, all of the index values would be zero. In this case, the status of fathers would be interacting with (or affecting) the status of sons to no degree at all. If, however, the status achieved by sons were absolutely dependent on the status of fathers there would be 100 percent interaction in all the cells of the table—a positive 100 in the cells of the left–to–right diagonal suggesting that the father's status was inevitably inherited by the son, a negative 100 elsewhere inasmuch as absolute status inheritance would preclude the son from any other status. Both of these extremes are unlikely situations. Let us contemplate an in–between scenario, one in which the status of the father merely weighted the odds against the son achieving any other status than the father's. For the sake of establishing a standard or model, we will assume that the son's freedom to advance (or fall) to a particular position by virtue of ability, luck, character and the like declined by half as the distance of that position from the father's increased. In such a situation we would obtain the lower set of values of the table. They are obviously not our index values. We have not, for one thing, allowed enough freedom of action at the middle level of society. Yet note the general similarity in pattern between the reality and the model. We are approximating in our scenario the situation in Middlesex.

Interaction indices applied to the whole sample give us a some-what rarified view of the operation of status in Middlesex. When the data are broken down according to the year in which sons came to maturity (presumed to be age twenty–one) and treated in the same fashion an element of movement is injected into the picture. Table 40, for example, depicts the interaction between the status of fathers and sons in the seventeenth century when white servitude prevailed and again in the period 1720-1750, by which time black slavery was in place in the county. In effect, we catch the society before and after the period of transition. The weak interaction at the middle levels seems a constant, while stronger indices along the diagonal of the lower table and in the quadrants where low and low middle intersect with high middle and high indicate an increasing stratification over time.

When we take another approach entirely the meaning of the indices in terms of the persons involved comes into focus. Once more we assign fathers and sons to status categories. Additionally we categorize them by land, labor, and estate, using time-specific category boundaries established by the natural clustering techniques

TABLE 40

Interaction of Status between Fathers and
Sons in Middlesex, 1650-1699, 1720-1750

Father's Status	Son's Status				
	Low	Low Middle	Middle	High Middle	High
1 6 5 0 - 1 6 9 9					
Low	14.3	-20.5	-11.0	-74.5	12.2
	9	*4*	*10*	*1*	*1*
Low Middle	6.4	28.6	15.0	-100.0	-100.0
	2	*3*	*5*	*0*	*0*
Middle	18.9	2.2	5.5	-6.8	-100.0
	11	*6*	*15*	*4*	*0*
High Middle	-89.3	-2.7	-2.0	25.7	-8.9
	1	*8*	*18*	*13*	*1*
High	-69.4	-100.0	-68.9	19.6	40.0
	1	*0*	*2*	*4*	*1*
1 7 2 0 - 1 7 5 0					
Low	30.0	3.6	16.4	-100.0	-100.0
	50	*8*	*2*	*0*	*0*
Low Middle	12.2	28.4	-34.9	-27.6	-100.0
	43	*19*	*1*	*1*	*0*
Middle	1.2	10.4	13.0	0.3	-100.0
	65	*27*	*5*	*3*	*0*
High Middle	-73.5	-69.6	4.3	56.5	-100.0
	17	*6*	*4*	*10*	*0*
High	-100.0	-100.0	-100.0	-100.0	100.0
	0	*0*	*0*	*3*	*2*

||*Source and Note*: See table 39. Sample sizes are given in italics in the second row of each category.

outlined in the previous section. (Table 27 illustrates in terms of the categorization of estates.)[19] Our concern remains the category of sons relative to fathers. But now we ask more personal questions. Did sons advance to a higher category? Fall to a lower? How many categories —analogous to rungs on a social ladder—separated sons from fathers? The overall results are depicted in figure 26. By any measure, roughly 40 to 50 percent of sons lost position relative to their fathers. When the gains and losses are refigured on the basis of the year the sons matured and broken down by the category of status, land, and labor into which fathers fell, the situation appears more complex. (Table 41.)

FIGURE 26

Son's Position Relative to Father's
in Middlesex, 1650–1750

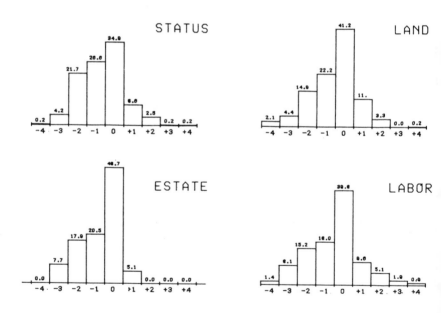

||*Source and Note*: The figure depicts the percent of sons remaining within the category of their fathers (0) and the percent falling (or rising) by one, two, three, and four categories from that of their fathers (+ and – 1,2,3,4). It is based on the sample described in table 39. Sample size: Status, land, labor 571; estate, 39.

TABLE 41

Status and Wealth of Middlesex Fathers
and Sons by Time

Father's Status	Of Sons Maturing					
	1650–1699		1720–1719		1720–1750	
	Percent Losing	Percent Gaining	Percent Losing	Percent Gaining	Percent Losing	Percent Gaining
STATUS						
Low	–	64.0	–	28.3	–	16.7
Low Middle	20.0	50.0	38.9	25.0	67.2	3.1
Middle	47.2	11.1	71.2	6.1	92.0	3.0
High Middle	65.9	2.4	75.0	7.1	73.0	0.0
High	75.0	–	50.0	–	60.0	–
LAND						
Low	–	50.0	–	23.4	–	20.9
Low Middle	17.4	47.8	33.3	30.6	52.5	5.1
Middle	33.9	23.2	69.4	6.9	71.9	4.5
High Middle	33.3	33.3	56.0	8.0	84.4	3.1
High	66.7	–	40.0	–	68.4	–
LABOR						
Low	–	55.6	–	35.1	–	10.9
Low Middle	53.8	38.5	50.0	31.3	78.6	7.1
Middle	39.3	25.0	64.0	12.0	83.9	3.3
High Middle	82.4	0.0	75.6	4.9	90.2	0.0
High	75.0	–	44.4	–	84.2	–

‖*Source and Note*: See table 39. Sample size by period: 120, 185, 266.
The sample of estates was too small to be disaggregated.

Over time, fewer and fewer sons managed to match the position
of their fathers, let alone improve on it. Sons of fathers of the lowest
strata ultimately found themselves virtually consigned to their
fathers' lot. Sixty-four percent of the sons of men of the lowest
status maturing in the seventeenth century were able to improve on
their father's position; only 17 percent of those maturing after 1719
and remaining in Middlesex did so. But it was the middling sort who
lost the most. Over half the sons of the middle-ranked fathers of
the seventeenth century held or improved upon their father's status;

over 90 percent of those maturing after 1719 lost. The phenomenon
was clearly a function of demography (the proclivity of fathers to
have more than one son), of diminishing resources as Middlesex
moved from an unsettled to a settled state, and of those changes in
the micro-economy resulting from slavery discussed in chapter 6.
Equally clearly, it amends the conclusion of our section on wealth.
There we wrote of the "Middling" sort growing both in relative size
and wealth. True enough. But sons of fathers of the middling sort,
becoming fathers, were finding it ever more difficult to gain for
themselves and their families the position and wealth of their youth—
that is to say, that of their fathers.

A word about occupation: Although it did not, in this essentially agricultural society, bulk large in the formal discriminant
analysis reported earlier in the sense that knowing the occupation
of a man did not contribute particularly to establishing status
within an aggregation, there are still insights to be gained from
occupation.

As might be expected, the vast majority of our Middlesex men
made at least a part of their livelihood from the land. But a surprising
number (17 percent of the sample we are using) combined agriculture
with other pursuits, while an additional 9 percent—all entering upon
their occupations in the eighteenth century—devoted themselves solely
to an occupation apart from agriculture.[20] The paramountcy of land
as an arbiter of a man's status and wealth clearly shows in table 42.
Here we have grouped men by their occupations (agricultural laborers,
building tradesmen, leather workers, proprietors, and the like), divided
each group into those combining planting with the occupation and
those wholly devoting themselves to the latter, and computed means
for our status index, land, labor, and estate.[21] In every instance,
exclusive adherence to a non-agricultural occupation lowered both the
mean of our status index and of the wealth variables.

We had anticipated that we would be able to locate specific
occupations on some sort of status continuum—building trades ranking
higher than leather workers, for example—but the effort failed. Given
small sample sizes, the differences within the central part of the tables
(the trades) are insignificant. The generally high position of the professional stands out, however; note that even without control of land,
professionals maintained a higher than average status. Merely the cur-
iosity of the visitors prompted table 43. Being essentially "teachers"
ourselves, we wondered how teachers fared in early Middlesex. The

TABLE 42

Status, Land, Labor, and Estate by Occupational
Groups in Middlesex, 1650–1750

Occupational Group	N	Mean			N	Mean Estate
		Status	Land	Labor		
Agricultural	18	1.7	169.7	1.4	7	85.1
Labor	*80*	*1.0*	*0.0*	*0.0*	*12*	*15.6*
Building	55	2.0	192.5	3.0	17	170.7
Trades	*27*	*1.4*	*32.7*	*1.1*	*2*	*15.0*
Leather	15	2.0	215.0	5.4	6	130.8
Trades	*6*	*1.3*	*16.7*	*0.2*	*1*	*36.0*
Food	15	2.0	110.7	4.2	5	134.0
Trades	*2*	*1.5*	*0.0*	*0.0*	*0*	–
Metal	8	2.1	453.8	3.9	2	105.0
Trades	*1*	*1.0*	*0.0*	*2.0*	*0*	–
Clothing	11	2.6	149.7	3.0	8	120.9
Trades	*8*	*1.4*	*43.8*	*0.4*	*6*	*17.7*
Plain Planter	772	2.0	257.0	3.1	181	152.9
Professional	31	3.1	551.1	9.2	11	192.5
	25	*3.0*	*95.8*	*3.1*	*2*	*84.5*
Proprietor	40	3.4	925.5	18.6	15	958.9
	12	*2.0*	*30.8*	*1.1*	*2*	*61.0*
Investor	22	4.0	2073.5	33.2	9	1332.6
	3	*3.7*	*0.0*	*4.3*	*1*	*850.0*

‖*Source and Notes*: See text for source and definitions. The upper figures
apply to individuals combining planting and the particular occupation, the lower
to those adhering exclusively to the occupation.

sample is small but the conclusion is so familiar as to have the
ring of truth about it. Teachers seem to have ranked among the
middling sort in terms of status, among the poorer sort in terms of
wealth.

Thus far women have not appeared in the analysis. As stated,
our data do not allow a direct assessment of female status. Still,

TABLE 43

Status and Wealth of Teachers and Other
Professionals in Early Middlesex

Group	% Teachers		% Other Professionals	
	In Status Group	In Estate Group	In Status Group	In Estate Group
Low	16.7	66.7	8.0	10.0
Low Middle	16.7	33.3	2.0	30.0
Middle	66.7	0.0	56.0	20.0
High Middle	0.0	0.0	34.0	40.0
High	0.0	0.0	0.0	0.0
Mean Status	2.5	–	3.2	–
Mean Estate	–	42.0	–	216.1
N	6	3	50	10

||*Source*: See text.

the question of the effect of what in chapter 1 we referred to as
social friction is too important to be ignored. How strong was the
sense of ordered hierarchy in our society? Specifically, was it
strong enough to affect marriage patterns? What were the effects of
other demonstrable phenomena—the scarcity of women in the early
population, the upward mobility of men who could (and did in so many
documented instances) rise in status and wealth by marrying heiresses
or widows, thereby gaining control of land?

We can at least approach such questions if we make certain
assumptions about status—assumptions neither invariably true nor
encompassing all of the relevant elements in the making of a marriage but adopted because of the intransigence of the data and the
importance of the problems. We will assume that the status of women
before their marriage derived from their fathers and after marriage
from their husbands. To enlarge the sample we will assume, further,
that if we do not know the status of a woman's father but know that
she was a servant prior to her first marriage, she began her freedom
with low status. Because of the nature by which, to this point, we
have assessed status we will have to make certain assumptions about
grooms as well. Status, recall, has been established as the highest

TABLE 44

Interaction of Status between Husbands and Wives
at Marriage in Middlesex, 1650-1699, 1720-1750

Husband's Status	Wife's Status				
	Low	Low Middle	Middle	High Middle	High

1 6 5 0 - 1 6 9 9

Husband's Status	Low	Low Middle	Middle	High Middle	High
Low	40.3	0.9	-0.6	-64.4	-100.0
	26	*7*	*20*	*5*	*0*
Low Middle	-100.0	19.3	34.4	-14.9	-100.0
	0	*1*	*4*	*1*	*0*
Middle	-5.4	9.9	2.3	14.1	-100.0
	3	*3*	*7*	*7*	*0*
High Middle	11.0	-20.3	-46.5	0.5	5.1
	8	*3*	*6*	*8*	*3*
High	-100.0	-100.0	-100.0	5.2	69.9
	0	*0*	*0*	*2*	*2*

1 7 2 0 - 1 7 5 0

Husband's Status	Low	Low Middle	Middle	High Middle	High
Low	19.4	5.2	17.5	-68.2	-100.0
	44	*28*	*37*	*4*	*0*
Low Middle	14.8	15.8	12.8	-73.9	-100.0
	24	*23*	*20*	*2*	*0*
Middle	3.9	16.2	15.2	-41.0	-100.0
	27	*36*	*33*	*7*	*0*
High Middle	-52.1	-48.8	-81.8	37.8	7.9
	3	*3*	*1*	*8*	*3*
High	-100.0	-100.0	-100.0	8.0	67.1
	0	*0*	*0*	*1*	*2*

‖*Source and Note*: See text for the derivation of the sample.
Interactive indices (see footnote 18) are entered in the first row of
each category, counts in the second.

status achieved by a male in life; at least in some instances that "highest status" was dependent upon the wife the man married inasmuch as she sometimes brought with her into the marriage land, personalty, even familial acceptance in the county. It would be erroneous, therefore, to use a male status perhaps dependent upon marriage to assess the role of status in the making of the marriage. We will have to assume that the groom's status at his first marriage also derived from his father (again assigning low status if the status of the father is unknown but the groom was a newly-freed servant) and ascribe to him his own achieved status only at the point of a second or subsequent marriage. Applying these assumptions to the data and

FIGURE 27

Status of Spouses of Low Status Males and Females
in Middlesex, 1650-1699

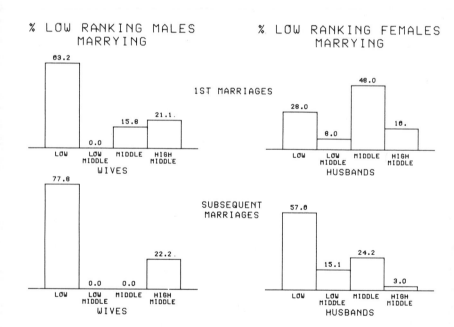

‖*Source and Note*: The figures are based on 19 first marriages involving low ranking males, 25 low ranking females, 18 widowers, 33 widows. See text for derivation of the sample and definitions.

FIGURE 28

Status of Spouses of Low Status Males and Females
in Middlesex, 1720–1750

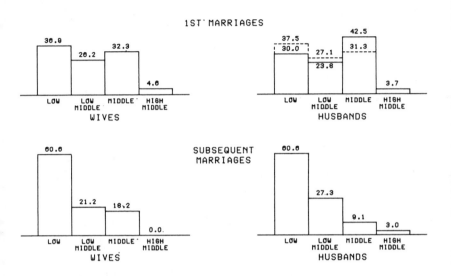

% LOW RANKING MALES
MARRYING

% LOW RANKING FEMALES
MARRYING

1ST MARRIAGES

WIVES

HUSBANDS

SUBSEQUENT
MARRIAGES

WIVES

HUSBANDS

‖*Source and Note:* Based on 65 marriages involving low ranking males,
80 low ranking females, 33 widowers, 33 widows. See text for derivation of the
sample and definitions. The broken lines and accompanying percentages in the
upper right figure depict the recalculation on the basis of the achieved
status of the groom rather than the status of the groom's father discussed
in the text.

extracting those marriages for which we can assess the status of both
bride and groom gives us a sample of 619 marriages for analysis.[22]

Table 44 displays results in terms of the interaction indices
described earlier, isolated into the periods 1650–1699 and 1720–1750
on the basis of the year of the marriage. Flaws in our assumptions
and the omission of crucial elements—was the groom already in pos-
session of a dead father's land? was the bride her father's heir or
simply a younger daughter?—bar all but large generalizations.[23] Two
are in order.

First, the interaction of status in the determination of a marriage partner is consistently strong at the highest level of the

status spectrum in Middlesex, and strengthens over time; indeed, in the later period the high and high middle ranks are, with regard to marriage, effectively separated from those lower down.

Second, and in contrast, relatively weak interaction where the lower three categories intersect indicates mobility among these groups, the one exception being the conjunction of low ranking brides and low ranking grooms in the earlier period. Figure 27 isolates the marriages among the lowest ranking males and females of the county in the earlier period and gives us additional insight. On the male side of the figure it is clear that low ranking males overwhelmingly took low ranking females in both their first marriages and as widowers. But the aspiring male who sought to advance by marrying upward is also clearly in evidence. The female side seems to reflect the shortage of women in the period with low ranking women free to advance themselves by marriage (or, conversely, middle ranking men freely taking them as wives).[24] Figure 28 isolates the same marriages for the later period. By then the low ranking males were taking wives roughly equally from the middle level downward but few from the high middle ranks and none from the high, reflecting the more general picture offered by the indices of table 44 among the lower levels and the increasing separation of the higher. In contrast, the strong upward mobility of females from low ranking families seems still in evidence. At first glance, the female figure suggests that upward mobility of women through marriage was less dependent upon a shortage of females than is generally thought. In actuality, however, the figure reflects the marriage of low ranking females to the sons of middle-ranking fathers who, in our assignment of status, received the rank of their fathers but were in reality slipping downward from it. When the figure is redone using the achieved status of the groom (that is to say, his own rather than his father's) it coincides almost exactly with the situation depicted for males.

|●|

1. Historians frequently use wealth as a surrogate for status simply because evidence of wealth is relatively easy to obtain. But in so doing they are silently accepting particular assumptions as to how societies function. The arguments of sociological theorists—from Marx and Weber, through Sorokin, Pareto, Parson, Dahrendorf, Lenski, and Tumin, to the present—are instructive. Lucile Duberman, *Social Inequality: Class and Caste in America* (New York, 1976) is a

convenient general introduction, Edwin R. Coover, "Socioeconomic Status and Structural Change," *Soc Sci. Hist.*, I (1977), 437–459 a good introduction to the complexities implicit in an historical analysis. In using the concept of "status" apart from "class" we are consciously following a line of development dating from Weber: "In contrast to the purely economically determined 'class situation,' we wish to designate as 'status situation' every typical component of the life fate of men that is determined by a specific, positive or negative, social estimation of honor." H. H. Gerth and C. Wright Mills, trans. and eds., *From Max Weber: Essays in Sociology* (New York, 1946), 186–187.

2. The last question is the very opposite of that of Shammas, "Constructing a Wealth Distribution," *Journ. Int. Hist.*, IX (1978), 297–307. She attempts to estimate wealth from what we construe as status variables.

3. We ranked male honorifics in the order: None, "Mister," "Gentleman," "Esquire." Four "Sirs" were subsumed with "Gentleman." Knighthood flowed along bloodlines and generated status of its own accord. The four fall naturally with "gentleman" on all variables.

4. In most cases occupation comes directly from a specification in one or more legal documents (e.g., "John Jones, Cooper"). "Planter" was affixed to the occupation if we knew an individual was indeed making a part of his living from the land. In a few cases we inferred occupation from activity. Only in this way could we establish such an occupation as "investor," a man who combined land speculation, factoring, merchandizing, local "banking," and the like.

5. Middlesex Orders, 1694–1705, 415; Middlesex Deeds, 1703–1720, 30.

6. The terminal date of the study required one further limit: The six adult years under observation had all to antedate 1750. Individuals for whom we could make no reasonable estimate of either land or labor (see "Wealth," note 9) were dropped.

7. A simple example of intuitive ranking is patroller as lower than constable, which is lower than sheriff.

8. Thus a surveyor of highways, who drew his authority directly from the county court, was ranked higher than an undersheriff, who drew his authority from the sheriff.

9. Hence the surveyor of highways with jurisdiction over six to eight miles of road in one relatively small segment of the county was ranked under a warehouse officer, who drew tobacco from roughly half the county. Any county-wide officer, of course, ranked higher than any intra-county officer, while any colony officer ranked higher than any county officer.

10. For brief definitions of *gamma* and the other measure of association used here (and their computation) see Norman H. Nie, et al., *SPSS*, 228, 230, 259–261, 280–281.

11. Many measures of association run from −1 through 0 to +1, the sign indicating the direction of the relationship. Pressure on a car brake and the speed of the car, for example, are negatively related (as brake pressure increases, speed decreases) and the appropriate measure of association (r) would be negative. We have, however, arranged all our ordinal scales in such a fashion as to produce only positive measures.

12. See Nie, et al., *SPSS*, 434–467.

13. The analysis requires that all cases in the set have values for all variables, that is, no missing data. As can be seen in the upper half of the matrix in table 31, this condition is met for the entire sample only for the five variables specified. In 299 cases we had data available for the five variables plus estate. When these 299 cases were analyzed separately, estate entered the calculations in the final (sixth) step and bulked least as a component of the first function derived (overwhelmingly a high office/honorific continuum) which in turn subsumed 95% of the variance. Estate was the principal element of a third function which subsumed less than 1% of the variance.

14. In this instance maximizing Rao's *V*, a criterion selected initially as a generalized distance measure. As it turned out, the criterion selected was of little consequence to the results.

15. The exact percentage (PJ = Petit Juror, EA = Estate Appraiser, GJ = Grand Juror, C = Constable, SH = Surveyor of Highways):

Office	PJ	EA	GJ	C	SH
Processioner	43.3	36.1	38.6	16.9	22.9
	1.3	*7.7*	*1.5*	*1.2*	*6.2*
Tobacco	73.3	73.3	56.7	33.3	60.0
Counter	*0.0*	*0.6*	*0.0*	*1.2*	*1.5*

The figures in italics (second row) are the obverse, e.g., 1.3% of petit jurors served earlier as processioners. Sixty percent of all tobacco counters had served earlier as processioners, 3.6% of all processioners as tobacco counters.

16. See chapter 5 for Provert.

17. Using a father's status as a base from which to measure the position of a son in a society with extraordinarily high orphanhood rates (see above under "Parental Loss") might seem hazardous, but in those instances in which we could establish a status for fathers, stepfathers, and guardians, it was clear that, from the vantage point of children, the status of the head of house remained roughly constant.

18. Technically, we transformed the values into doubly-standardized ratios (following Stephen E. Fienberg, "A Statistical Technique for Historians: Standardizing Tables of Counts," *Journ. Int. Hist.*, I (1971), 305–315) and computed residuals by subtracting from the ratios the common cell value expected assuming independence. Neither doubly-standardized ratios nor residuals carry strong intuitive meaning, hence we took the computations one step further. The common cell value assuming independence (1 / NR where NR is the number of columns in a symmetrical table) governs the range of potential residuals; they can vary from 0 – (1 / NR) through 1 – (1 / NR). Thus in a 5 by 5 table we expect a common cell value assuming independence of 0.2 and the residuals can range from –0.2 through 0.8. We convert the residuals to a percent of all possible negative or positive interaction by dividing them by the minimum of the range and subtracting from zero if negative, by the maximum if positive. In table 39, for example, the datum in the cell defined by the first row, first column (97) converts to a doubly-standardized ratio of 0.399, a residual of 0.199, and an interaction index of 0.248—that is, 24.8% of all potential positive interaction. During the past few years statisticians have found technical weaknesses in doubly-standardized ratios and devised superior methods for isolating interaction; were we to go beyond broad suggestions and into an extensive ransacking

of such tables—Leo A. Goodman's word in "How to Ransack Social Mobility Tables and Other Kinds of Cross-Classification Tables," *American Journal of Sociology*, LXXV (1969-1970), 1-40—their sophisticated procedures would be in order. See e.g., Robert M. Hauser, "A Structural Model of the Mobility Table," *Social Forces*, LVI (1977-1978), 919-953; Robert McCaa, "Modeling Social Interaction: Marital Miscegenation in Colonial Spanish America," *Hist. Methods*, XV (1982), 45-66.

19. Using such clustering minimizes the effect of a changing norm. It has been well established that in any early American locale the amount of land held by individuals tended to decline as density rose over time. See e.g., Darrett B. Rutman, "People as Process: The New Hampshire Towns of the Eighteenth Century," *Journal of Urban History*, I (1975), 268-292; Kenneth A. Lockridge, "Land, Population and the Evolution of New England Society, 1630-1790," *Past & Present*, XXXIX (1968), 62-80; James T. Lemon, *The Best Poor Man's Country: A Geographical Study of Early Southeastern Pennsylvania* (Baltimore, Md., 1972), 93-94. Categorizing holdings into such groups as high, middle, low must conform to this phenomenon. A man with 100 acres at a time and place where the average was 500 might be appropriately labeled "low"; at a time and place where the mean holding was 100, however, "low" would certainly be inappropriate. The man's holding did not change, only the distribution within which the holding is to be categorized.

20. Of the 1,653 in the sample defined earlier, we could establish occupations for 1,171, of whom 772 (65.9%) were planters only, 98 (8.3%) were agricultural laborers, and 301 (25.7%) either combined another occupation with planting (198 or 16.9%) or wholly devoted themselves to an occupation apart from agriculture (103 or 8.8%).

21. For the most part the grouping is self-explanatory. It is modeled on that of Michael B. Katz, "Occupational Classification in History," *Journ. Int. Hist.*, III (1972), 63-68, with adjustments appropriate to the shift from the mid-nineteenth century to the early Chesapeake. And we have broken skilled trades apart for the purpose outlined in the text. Agricultural laborers include overseers, sharecroppers, and hired laborers. Professionals include attorneys, ministers, clerks, doctors, surgeons, farriers, and teachers. Among proprietors we placed those we could identify as storekeepers, millowners, ordinary keepers, ferry owners, and what today would be called "contractors," men who regularly ran crews of carpenters and undertook the construction of houses and public buildings on contract. "Investor" is the most awkward category, comparable perhaps to Katz's "gentleman." It includes factors and those for whom we could identify a multiplicity of investments in goods, ships, and land. We have excluded seamen and a miscellaneous category—peddlers and musicians, for example—from the analysis.

22. An additional forty-four marriages in which the status of the new bride or remarrying widow could be established were with men from beyond the county. These have been omitted from consideration. Two-thirds of all high status women in the sample married out of the county. By way of contrast, 19% of high middle women did so, and only 5% of the middle, low middle, and low status women, most from the upper part of the county (where there was no natural barrier between Middlesex and Essex) and the lower precinct (where the Piankatank proved a somewhat permeable barrier).

23. Our attempts to disaggregate marriages further to take such things into account resulted in samples too small for analysis. Indeed, in many instances the resulting argument would have ceased to be statistical and become all but ad hominem.

eleven

LITERACY

In compiling the Middlesex biographies described in chapter 1 we recorded two variables which, we hoped, would shed light upon literacy in the county. The first was that classically used to measure literacy in the absence of other data— signatures. Did a person sign a name to a document or simply "make a mark." The relationship of measured signatures to true literacy is obviously complex and essentially unknown. Among early American historians, Kenneth A. Lockridge has written most lucidly on the problem.[1] There is no need for us to repeat his argument. Suffice it to say that our second variable involved an attempt to break free of the inherent limitations of a signature analysis. We recorded, when we found it, any positive evidence of literacy or illiteracy. Was a person engaged professionally or as a friend to prepare a document for another? Was there a holograph document written by the indivi- dual—a letter, journal, contract, legal plea? We took such things as positive evidence of a literate person. Did an individual specifically state that he or she was literate or illiterate, perhaps in a deposition or, by implication, in citing a book that he or she had read?

In the end we had data of some sort on 2,090 individuals, 1,611 men and 479 women. Table 45 summarizes our counts on the two variables

TABLE 45

Evidence of Literacy in Middlesex
by Time

Sex	N	Percent of Individuals			
		Known Literate	Signing	Marking	Known Illiterate
		1650 - 1699			
Male	601	11.5	53.1	35.4	0.0
Female	124	3.2	29.8	66.9	0.0
		1700 - 1750			
Male	990	12.0	58.8	28.9	0.3
Female	348	0.6	26.4	72.7	0.3
		ALL CASES			
Male	1611	11.7	56.9	31.2	0.2
Female	479	1.3	27.8	70.8	0.2

||*Source and Notes*: See text for source. The total sample is broken down by
date of death in the county or disappearance from its records.

and breaks down the counts according to the century (seventeenth or eighteenth) in which the individual died or disappeared
from our records. The eighteenth century breakdown allows a direct
comparison with Lockridge's findings for the Chesapeake. In analyzing signatures on 437 male wills, 1705–1762, he found signatures
on 66 percent, marks on 34 percent.[2] When we combine signatures and known literacy (on the grounds that the literate would
have signed rather than marked) our equivalent percentages for the
eighteenth century are 71 and 29.[3]

Table 45 also indicates the failure of our attempt to break
through the conceptual difficulties of a signature analysis with a
new type of evidence. In the end we had too little direct evidence
of illiteracy to be useful—four cases in all, all from the eighteenth
century. Evidence of known literacy among males was more plentiful
and invariably followed secular trends in the signature counts, vali-
dating to an extent conclusions as to trends based upon the latter.
But the material offered little beyond that. And the abrupt decline

Literacy

FIGURE 29

Percent Literate within Status Groups
in Middlesex by Time (Males)

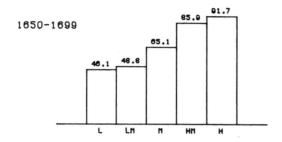

1650-1699

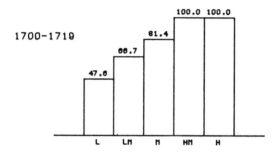

1700-1719

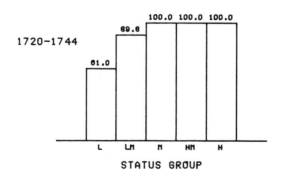

1720-1744

STATUS GROUP

‖*Source and Note*: See text for source and definitions of the status groups.
L = Low, LM = Low Middle, M = Middle, HM = High Middle, H = High. The dates
represent the period in which subjects came to maturity (age 21). Sample sizes
by period are 587, 254, 224 respectively.

in known female literacy in the eighteenth century seems less related
to literacy in fact and more an artifact of, hence evidence of, the
eighteenth-century retirement of women into the household (and away
from the sorts of materials upon which our study is based) about
which others have speculated.[4] In any event, with little to be gained
from the new evidence we have simply subsumed known literacy and
illiteracy into the signature data.

TABLE 46

Literacy by Occupational Group in
Middlesex, 1650–1750

Occupational Group	N	Percent Signing
Professional	53	100.0
Investor	25	100.0
Proprietor	45	88.9
Metal Trades	8	87.5
Food Trades	15	80.0
Building Trades	60	68.3
Clothing Trades	14	64.3
Plain Planter	603	60.0
Leather Trades	13	53.8
Former Servant	120	46.7
Agric. Laborer	52	38.4

‖*Source:* See table 42. We have
added a literacy rate for men
identifiable as former servants.

Figure 29 depicts the growth of literacy among males in the
county over time and by the status groups developed in the last
section. The familiar phenomenon of literacy growing from the top
down is clearly apparent. For its part, table 46 elaborates upon
table 42, adding a literacy percentage to the various occupational
groups depicted earlier. We have also inserted within the table a
literacy figure computed for men known to have served as servants—
47 percent literate, compared to 60 percent for the plain planters,
65 percent for the table overall less the former servants.

Figure 30 is germane when one considers the source of literacy
as against simply describing groups according to literacy. Literacy
might contribute to a man's status, but status in and of itself does
not contribute to his literacy; that he in all likelihood gained as a
boy or young man, and the availability of the wherewithal for
instruction would depend upon the environment provided by parents,

FIGURE 30

Male and Female Literacy in Middlesex
by Father's Status and Time

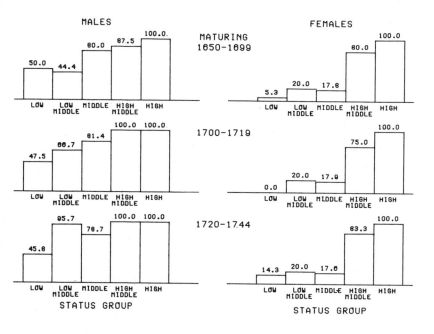

‖*Source and Notes*: See text for source and the definition of the status categories. The dates represent the period in which subjects came to maturity (21 for males, 18 for females). Sample sizes by period are 102, 254, and 162 (males) and 96, 50, 46 (females).

which in turn is related to *their* status. This last we can only approach from the standpoint of the father and, in figure 30, we depict the percentage of sons and daughters of Middlesex literate by the status of the father, broken down into three periods by assigning the sons and daughters to one or another period according to the year they came to maturity—presumed to be eighteen in the case of females, twenty-one in the case of males. With one exception the figure depicts a familiar lineal relationship between literacy and father's status. The exception is the enhanced percentage of literate sons of low-status fathers in the last period (perhaps echoed among their daughters, although the sample is too small to be sure). The unexpected enhancement could be an artifact—a quirk in the data or in our procedures—although it appears again when we resort to our wealth indices. When, for example, fathers are categorized by their land,[5] 94 percent of the sons of those falling in the low-middle category maturing in this period were literate by our signature method as against but 57 percent of the sons of low category fathers and 85 percent of sons of middle-category fathers. It almost seems that eighteenth-century fathers of the lower middle rank in Middlesex, to a greater extent than others, urged literacy upon their children, perhaps because they themselves had grown up in higher ranked households. In this regard the conclusion drawn earlier is is pertinent: Over time the sons of fathers of the middling sort in Middlesex were finding it ever more difficult to gain for themselves and their families the position of their own youth as reflected in their fathers' status and wealth.

|●|

1. Kenneth A. Lockridge, *Literacy in Colonial New England: An Enquiry into the Social Context of Literacy in the Early Modern West* (New York, 1974).

2. Ibid., 77. Note that while Lockridge used only wills, we used any document to establish the form of a signature.

3. Our data were recorded using a single code, viz., positive evidence of literacy = 1; signs = 2; marks = 3; positive evidence of illiteracy = 4. We found no case in which positive evidence was contradicted by the form of signature.

4. E.g., Lois Green Carr and Lorena S. Walsh, "The Planter's Wife: The Experience of White Women in Seventeenth-Century Maryland," *WMQ*, 3d Ser., XXXIV (1977), 567-571. The same retirement probably accounts for the decline in female sample sizes in figure 29.

5. As in table 34.

twelve

THE AGGREGATE BLACK

Earlier, under "Population Estimates,"
we outlined the way in which we established the size of the black
population of Middlesex and its rate of growth. Here we are
concerned with its composition.

Immediately we must stress the tentativeness of anything we conclude. Insofar as the historian is concerned, the blacks of Middlesex
lived their lives in the anonymity of being construed property. Our
way has been to reconstruct the lives of men and women on the basis
of the bits and pieces of paper they left behind, then extract from
the set of reconstructions aggregations significant enough to carry
the burden of a statistical analysis. The black, being property and
illiterate, left nothing on his own volition. He could not sue or be
sued, hence left behind no writs or pleas or appearances. His marriages went unrecorded. He could hold no office. He sat on no juries.
Indeed, only on rare occasions could he testify before the justices.
Property himself, he could not deal in property, hence left no trail
of commercial paper for us to unravel. All that we really have on
record about the black is what the white society, in its own interest,
thought worth recording. A black newly arrived from Africa or the
Caribbean would be taxable or not according to his (or her) age; if

a particular slave looked young enough, it was in the interest of the owner to conform to the law and bring the slave before the justices to have his or her age adjudged and recorded:

> Charlott A Negro Girl Belonging to Henry
> Thacker is adjudged to be twelve years
> of Age.[1]

The appearance or disappearance of slave property was important for tax purposes, too, hence there was a tendency to record slave births and deaths:

> Monmouth Son of Sharlott a Slave
> belonging to Henry Thacker born
> September the 11. 1722[2]

The recording, however, was erratic—spotty in the early years, fairly regular from roughly 1720 into the 1740s, then spotty again. Slaves, as property, were bequeathed in wills (as Sharlott was left to Henry Thacker's widow, Mary Elizabeth, in 1764).[3] And they were included in the inventories made of a decedent's estate. Given patience, care, and a readiness to admit the potential for error, such entries can sometimes be linked together to outline the life of a slave. Our sketch of Thacker's Sharlott and her descendants in chapter 6 is an example. But we are not able to do this confidently with enough cases to allow the sort of analysis of mortality or fertility which we have done for the white population.

Nevertheless, it is imperative that we have at least some idea of certain aspects of black life in the county. If we cannot devise a mortality schedule for the black, we still must know something about the length of the black's working life. If we cannot describe the black population in terms of customary age categories, we still need a rough notion of the size of the working population relative to those too young or too old to work. The economic strategies of the whites in an era of black labor, and white success or failure, depended largely upon such phenomena.

Our search for answers to these questions drew us to descriptions of slaves compiled from the extant Middlesex records, most frequently from inventories and other documents associated with probate but occasionally from conveyances, mortgages, trial records, adjudgments of age, and the like. The very fullest descriptions include three discrete bits of information: an age, a value, and a descriptive word or phrase—"sucking child," "boy," "lusty wench," "old." For the most part, however, any single description contained only one or some combination of two of these pieces rather than all three. How fully we could use the descriptions depended upon how much of what was missing we could estimate.

A series of logical postulates guided the process of estimation. The value of a slave was related to the profit to be obtained from the slave's labor (productivity) and through productivity to sex and

FIGURE 31

Age Ranges of Slaves Described by Particular
Phrases in Middlesex, 1650–1750

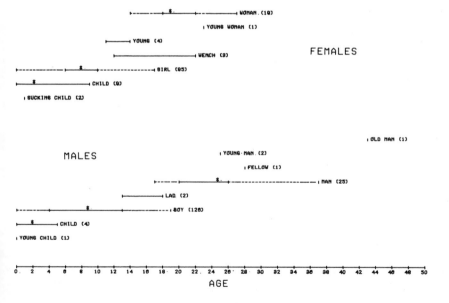

Source and Notes: See text for source. The solid and broken lines together indicate the full range of ages associated with the descriptive word or phrase. Where the data allow, the broken lines indicate the tails of a distribution, (top and bottom one-sixth of the cases), the asterisk the mean. The value in parentheses represents the number of cases.

FIGURE 32

Value Ranges of Slaves Described by Particular
Phrases in Middlesex, 1650–1750

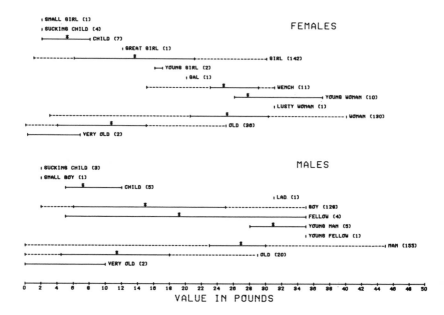

||*Source and Notes*: See figure 31.

age. The labor of a female slave was less productive than that of a
male, hence females were valued less than males of comparable age,
although to some extent this was mitigated by the fact that the
female was at least the potential mother of additional slaves. The
relationship between value and age was curvilinear; slaves had greatest value at their most productive ages and least value when, in
infancy and again in old age, their productivity was negligible or
non-existent. These relationships have been amply demonstrated for
the nineteenth century by, among others, Robert Fogel and Stanley
Engerman.[4] They are easily demonstrated in empirical data from
Middlesex.

Consider the words used to describe slaves. We can fix the age
implied by such descriptors by looking at those cases for which we

have both a descriptor and an age. In figure 31 the range of ages associated with various descriptors is depicted. One hundred and twenty-six "boys," for example, ranged in age from zero (that is, birth to first birthday) through nineteen. Where we have enough cases to allow a meaningful computation, the mean is indicated (for "boys," 8.8), as is the range of the middle two-thirds of the cases (ages four through thirteen for the category "boy")[5]. The relationship of the descriptors to specific age groups is immediately apparent. "Child," "boy," "lad," "man," "old man," are clearly describing ascending age groups. Figure 32 depicts in the same way the ranges and central tendencies of the values associated with various descriptors. To use "boy" again as an example: 128 boys ranged in value from 2/i through 35/i, averaging 15/i; two-thirds of the cases fell between 6/i and 25/i. Again, the specificity of the descriptors shows itself: Boys are of less value than "men"; "young" is an adjective isolating a sub-category of "man" or "woman" of greater value than an unmodified "man" or "woman."[6] The relationship between descriptors, age, value, and sex is even clearer in figure 33. The curves depicting male and female values by age (as suggested by the descriptors) are near duplicates of nineteenth-century curves based upon much more precise and fuller data.

Figure 34, too, suggests the familiar curves, but only vaguely. Here the ranges of values associated with male and female slaves of particular ages are plotted (the solid lines), with the mean of the value indicated by an asterisk. (Asterisks plotted apart from range lines indicate single cases.) The upslopes of the curves are clear enough—value increasing as age increases, with both males and females entering into their period of peak value around age eighteen. Indeed, the data at this end of the age distribution are strong enough to compute a meaningful regression line, idealizing the relationship between age and value through age twenty.[7] But the paucity of our data hides the downslopes. From roughly age twenty we have only a scattering of cases for which we have certain knowledge of both age and value.

The age-specific nature of the descriptive words and the strong relationship between age and value through age twenty open two avenues to estimation. Bess, for example, was a "girle" on Ralph Wormeley's Robinson's Quarter evaluated at twelve pounds in the 1701 inventory of Wormeley's estate.[8] We know that "girl" implied a female of a particular age, hence the chances are that Bess was between six

FIGURE 33

Differential Values of Male and Female Slaves Using Means
of Values and Ages Associated with Descriptive Phrases

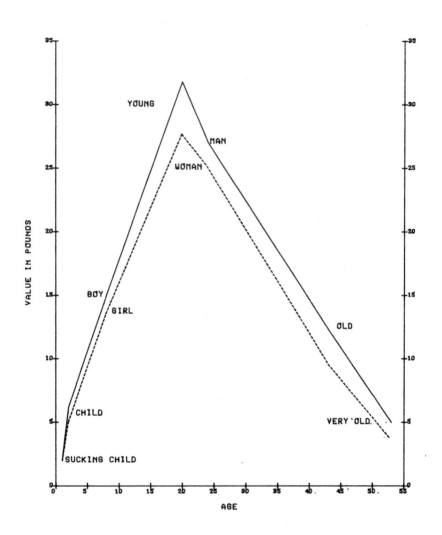

||*Source*: See text and figures 31 and 32.

by standardizing values to a base year.[10] For this purpose we have assumed a 5 percent overall inflation between 1700 and 1723, 49 per cent from 1723 through 1745, and set 1723 as our base.[11] Adjusting Bess's 1701 value to the 1723 base (her 12/*i* is corrected to 12.6) and using a regression of deflated values on age allow us to estimate her age at roughly eight.[12]

The use of values to estimate unknown ages where a descriptor implies an age less than or equal to twenty is our strongest procedure. It gives us additional cases at the younger ages, but also a few additions to the downslope of figure 34, for in some instances we have slaves evaluated as "girls" or "boys" at one point in time and as "women" or "men" at another. The fact that we can estimate the age at the earlier point in time allows us to fix a point estimate at a later. Where we have no value at all, only a descriptor—one with a relatively narrow range of ages associated with it—we can obtain a weaker estimate by fixing upon a particular value within the range.[13] Even using both procedures, however, we are still without enough cases to fix the relationship of age and value beyond age twenty. We have had to resort to another bit of information.

In eighty-seven instances of females for whom we have no age (either empirical or estimated by one of the processes already described) we have a least some knowledge as to childbirths. Della, for example, was described in 1728 as part of the estate of Thomas Haslewood. The inventory offers us nothing other than a value of twenty-five pounds.[14] No age is given. No descriptor is attached to her name. However, we know of children born to Della between 1717 and 1727. This additional information suggests that Della was probably no younger than twenty-seven nor older than forty-six. If she were younger than twenty-seven in 1728, the earliest child we know of would have been born when she was fifteen or under—possible, of course, but not particularly probable. If she were older than forty-six, the last child we know of would have been born after she was forty-five—again, possible but not probable. The range of known childbirths, in effect, sets rough boundaries to female age at the time of an evaluation. But we need point estimates rather than ranges, hence must make a definitive assumption as to the relationship between age and known childbirths. We could assume that the first child was born when Della was indeed at the start of her fertile years (sixteen) or that the last child was born at the very end of those years (forty-five); either assumption would fix her age in 1728. But were we to apply such assumptions generally to our problem of estimating ages, the first would lead to a bias toward a young population, the second to an older one.

Our solution was to assume that at the mid-point of a known childbearing range (1722 in Della's case) the woman in question was at the mid-point of her childbearing years (thirty years old). By this reasoning Della was thirty-six when she was valued at twenty-five pounds. Applied generally when all other attempts to estimate age failed, we finally arrived at enough cases to complete (at least for females) a full age-value curve. The female curve of figure 35, based upon 110 cases in which we knew the age and 238 in which the age was estimated in one fashion or another, depicts the results in terms of a six degree polynomial fitted to the data points.[15] The concomitant male curve was arrived at by applying the male-female differentials suggested by figure 33. Both male and female curves became the basis for one final effort to establish ages still unestimated. By way of example, consider an evaluation (adjusted for inflation to the base year 1723) of twenty pounds for a female described only as a "woman." We know nothing more about her. Yet the descriptor tells us that she was in all probability on the down- rather than up-side of the age-price curve; on that side, a value of twenty pounds equates to roughly thirty-seven—our estimate.

Our purpose throughout these manipulations was to form a data base which would allow us to gain a sense of the composition of the slave population of Middlesex. In the end we had available 1,352 cases—slaves of at least an estimated age observed for the most part (over 90 percent) in the eighteenth century. Some phenomena were immediately apparent in this data. A slave, male or female, was viewed as "old" from the early forties onward, as "very old" from the early fifties; a "prime" hand, again male or female, was one between the late teens and late thirties, an age span covering just twenty years. Before going beyond the obvious, however, we must make a short excursion into demographic possibilities.

Let us contemplate a single cargo of blacks arriving in the Chesapeake. If the cargo had been bought by a single planter and

---

||*Source and Note*: See text for source. The shaded area approximates the percentage African-born.

The Aggregate Black

FIGURE 36

Successive Age Structures Flowing from a Single Hypothetical
Slave Cargo Entering the Chesapeake

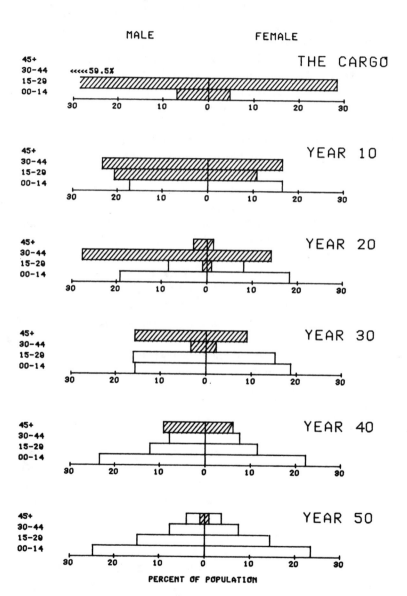

placed in one location, with no slaves ever being removed by the
planter nor new slaves added, what would have been the resulting
slave population after the passage of a number of years? The situation is obviously artificial. We have contrived a closed population in
order to apply the mathematics of demography—the fundamental
relationships between age, mortality, and fertility—to establish parameters within which the black population actually developed.

The best historical evidence suggests that the cargo would consist of a handful of children through age fourteen and a large number
of young adult males and females, with males outnumbering females
by a ratio of two to one. Weak from the journey and entering a new
disease environment, a number of the newcomers would die soon after
arrival. Strong evidence, moreover, suggests that conditions of health
and nutrition, possibly even the social conditions inherent in the situation, would depress the fertility of the women; they would, on average,
have fewer children than their descendants in America, perhaps their
mothers in Africa. Yet even depressing their fertility by 30 percent,
the very fact of so large a part of the female population being within
their fertile years (86 percent) would result in children and population
growth, at least for a few years. Only as mortality and the passage
of time took their toll, the first by removing fertile women from the
population, the second by edging the survivors into years of lower and
lower fertility while their daughters were still pre-pubescent, would
population growth cease. And only as the native born daughters took
husbands and had children of their own would growth set in again.
Figure 36 depicts this process in terms of successive age pyramids
while table 47 isolates key statistics: the sex and child-woman
ratios, and the proportion of the population African and "prime,"
the last defined generously as the proportion ages fifteen through
forty-four.[16]

Our hypothetical situation—our model—suggests what we are likely
to see in Middlesex itself, but only to an extent. The prism through
which we view the reality in the county—the descriptions and the
estimated ages we must use—inevitably distorts. Equally to the point,
reality has a way of clouding the purity of any model. Constants
encompassed in the model—the sex and age distribution of slave
cargoes, fertility and mortality rates—are in actuality inconstant. There
are variables which the model does not encompass. Our simulation, for
example, traces developments from the arrival of a single cargo. But
there were blacks in Middlesex from the very beginning of settlement,

TABLE 47

Successive Population Statistics Flowing from a Single
Hypothetical Slave Cargo Entering the Chesapeake

Year	Population	Males per Female	Children 0-4 per Woman 15-46	Proportion 15-44		Proportion African
				Male	Female	
Cargo	150	2.0	0.00	0.60	0.29	1.00
5	157	1.7	0.81	0.52	0.25	0.80
10	167	1.6	0.79	0.44	0.22	0.66
15	168	1.5	0.67	0.39	0.19	0.57
20	168	1.4	0.55	0.36	0.22	0.48
25	172	1.3	0.76	0.26	0.19	0.39
30	179	1.2	0.99	0.20	0.17	0.30
35	187	1.2	1.02	0.19	0.18	0.22
40	196	1.1	0.95	0.20	0.19	0.15
45	204	1.1	0.87	0.23	0.22	0.09
50	214	1.1	0.92	0.23	0.22	0.03
75	333	1.0	0.93	0.22	0.21	0.00
100	523	1.0	0.93	0.22	0.21	0.00

||*Source*: See text.

most brought in from York by major families such as the Wormeleys.
The start of large scale importations in the 1680s added to an existing population rather than initiated a brand new one. And significant
infusions of new blacks came at a number of points in time rather
than only once—in the 1680s and again in the 1690s, in the mid-years
of the first decade, in 1719 and 1721. In the 1720s and 1730s, moreover, a series of epidemics struck the black population. One in 1721
was particularly hard on children. Another, extending from 1726
through 1728, seems to have left children alone while striking down
adults. Still another in 1737 hit at all age groups but particularly
at adolescents and young blacks.[17]

The demography of the model, successive surges of importations,
and epidemics all show in the series of age pyramids shown in
figure 37. The pyramids are based upon five-year aggregations of
the blacks whose descriptions we have been using, a procedure
designed to balance the necessity for a time-specific sample with
the need for the largest possible representation of the black
population. Those drawn on the basis of descriptions of 1698–1702
and 1708–1712 are marked by predominant 15–29 age groups, as one

might expect given the pattern of importations.[18] Yet the existence
of long-time black residents is indicated by the relatively large
number of older blacks in 1698–1702 and the exceptionally low sex
ratio.[19] Ten years later these indicators have all but disappeared,
testimony to the massiveness of the slave importations of the first
decade of the century. By 1718–1722 the effect of so many years
during which so large a part of the population was at peak fertility
shows clearly. Children 0–14 predominate in the population. Indeed,
there are over three such children for every woman 15–44. The aging
Africans of the early years of the century, their daughters not
yet in the full bloom of childbearing, are suggested in the fourth
pyramid. The fifth bears the marks of the epidemics, the loss of
children in that of 1721 and of adolescents and young adults in
1737 having sorely depleted the 15–29 year old category.

There is, of course, an innate importance to the demography of
the black population of the county. Scholars such as Allan Kulikoff
begin their efforts to comprehend the life of the slave with such
figures.[20] And while we have been able to use slightly more refined
procedures, our results are not very different from those of others,
a similarity tending to substantiate what is becoming a common
understanding of the early black population.[21] Yet understanding the
effect of the black upon the white is as important as understanding
the black experience itself. Such understanding, too, begins with
demography, but moves quickly into economics.

Let us return to our hypothetical planter buying a single cargo
of blacks and putting them to labor upon one location. Essentially
his is an economic act. He intends profit. Is he successful? The
general question resolves itself into four specific questions. He has
purchased the cargo, whether with cash or credit. How quickly does
he recover his original investment? At any given point in time his
slaves constitute the largest part of his current capital. (Land constitutes most of the rest.) This part of his capital is forever changing.
Slaves are added (by virtue of births) and subtracted (deaths).
In any given year, how does his current slave capital compare to
his original investment? What is his yearly profit? This, too,

||Source: See text.

would change, for as his slaves move toward or away from prime age,
their productivity, hence the size of his crop and profit, changes.
Finally, what is his rate of return on capital in any given year?
Are his slaves a good investment, or would he be better off selling
out and putting his money elsewhere? Figure 38 summarizes our
answers.[22]

By the end of the tenth year following his purchase our planter
would recoup the cost of the original cargo out of yearly profits.
Current capital as represented by the slave force would not soon
regain the level of the original investment, however. Indeed, throughout the remainder of our planter's life, inexorable demographic factors
would erode slave capital, annual profit, even the planter's return on
current capital. For note in table 47 that on first settling the cargo
upon his land our planter could count on less than maximum labor
(and hence less than maximum profit) from only 11 percent of his
hands, all children. Thirty-four years later children and old people
among the slaves would amount to 64 percent of the total, prime
hands only 36 percent. The percent of prime hands would recover from
this nadir, settling at around 44 percent of the slave force. The
growth of the force itself would, between the forty-second and fifty-
fifth years, reverse the generally downward slopes of our indices.
Current slave capital and annual profit would steadily rise while
return on capital would stabilize at about 7.3 percent—all to the
benefit of our original planter's children and grandchildren.[23] Some-
time in their lifetimes, moreover, the size of the labor force would
cease to be the major determinant of profit. The area of our hypothetical plantation, while unspecified, has been considered a constant.
Given the demography of the situation it would ultimately be too
small and the blacks would have to be siphoned away and set to work
elsewhere, or be given work other than tending tobacco.

All of the drawbacks associated with the original demographic
model, and then some, apply to this economic model. Its very
sparseness, however, allows us to see quite clearly the probable
effects of real situations. Let us assume that our hypothetical
planter was a Middlesex man and the cargo was imported in 1700. As
it stands, he would, in 1740, be making a profit of roughly 183/*l*
on slave capital of almost 3,000/*l*, a 6.1 percent return. Yet the
heightened mortality of the epidemic years would cost him slaves and
change the age structure of the labor force, and these in turn would
have an effect on his economic situation. When we proceed to "tune"

FIGURE 38

Simulated Returns on an Investment in Slavery

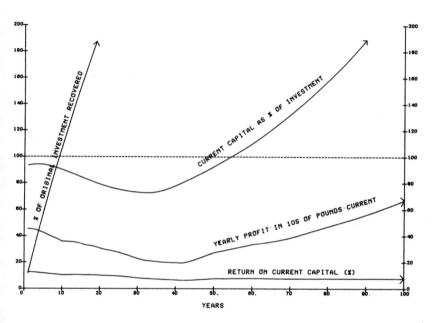

YEARS

||*Source*: See text.

the model by entering the epidemics into the calculations we reduce his capitalization in 1740 to just below 2,100/*i*, his profit to 122/*i*, and his return to 5.8 percent. The pure model proceeds on the assumption of a static economy in which tobacco prices never change, costs remain constant, and slave values at the various ages are unvarying. In reality inflation marked the economy of the eighteenth-century Chesapeake, with the price trend rising slowly during the years to 1723, then faster. But in Middlesex tobacco prices were a significant exception. Having reached a plateau in the first decade of the century (see table 1), the price of Middlesex's sweetscented, while varying, remained in terms of trends relatively constant. When the model is tuned to reflect not only the epidemics but rising costs, rising slave values, and constant tobacco prices, the results again shift. In 1740 our hypothetical planter's capital in slaves would once more be approaching 3,000*li* (the inflation of slave values mitigating the effect of the epidemics) but profit would have sunk to 84*li* and return on capital to 3.1 percent (reflecting higher capitalization, higher costs, and constant tobacco prices).

Obviously we cannot accept as definitive the finite numbers produced by the model. Specific results flow from the entry of specific numbers into the calculations, but the numbers are themselves inexact. Did 5 percent of the children die in the children's epidemic of 1721? Or 7 percent? Or 10 percent? Neither can we apply the model unvaryingly to individual planters. They did not buy slaves in cargo-lots and set them down to work tobacco for a hundred years. The model simply gives us insight into complicated interrelationships. And these lead to a number of general conclusions. County-wide, the profitabiltiy of slavery would be at its peak in the years immediately following the massive importations of the first decade of the eighteenth century, when the proportion of prime blacks was high and the proportion children and old relatively low. The fact that a basically African work force would have to be trained to its labor might mitigate this conclusion but does not negate it. The epidemics of the 1720s and 1730s would adversely affect the accumulation of slave capital. And the inflation of the century, combined with constant prices for sweetscented tobacco, would increase the real value of the planters' slaves (capital) but decrease their return on capital and real profit. All of these general movements would play upon the fortunes of individuals within our county.

|●|

1. Middlesex Orders, 1710–1721, 481.

2. *Register of Christ Church*, 209.

3. Middlesex Wills, 1675–1798, Pt. 2, 334–335.

4. Robert William Fogel and Stanley L. Engerman, *Time on the Cross: The*

Economics of American Negro Slavery (Boston, 1974), 72–77, idem, *Time on the Cross: Evidence and Methods—A Supplement* (Boston, 1974), 80–85.

5. Roughly bounding one standard deviation on either side of the mean. The distributions in every instance approximate normality.

6. The strength of the categorizations depicted in figures 31 and 32 has been tested through a one-way analysis of variance. 66.6% of the variation in male ages and 63.2% of that in female ages is encompassed by the categorization (reporting *eta*-squared converted to a percent of total sum-of-squares between categories). Similarly, 45.1% of the variation in male values and 51.9% of that in female values is encompassed. All results are significant at better than the 0.001 level. The weaker fit of values to the categories is largely a function of the use of raw data, that is, values uncorrected for inflation. When deflated values are used (see below), the fit of values to categories matches that of age to categories.

7. Specifically a regression line with an intercept of 2.238 and slope of 1.567 (female) and 4.307 and 1.479 (male). The regression, with age as the independent variable, was computed with 110 female and 110 male cases and accounted for 87.2 and 78.5 percent of the variation respectively (reporting r-squared multiplied by 100).

8. Middlesex Wills, 1698–1713, 129.

9. By the computation $(V - A) / B$ where V is the value, A the intercept, and B the slope.

10. Because of the strong relationship between value and age, the changing age structure of the slave population confounds the effort to isolate trends. The following table, for example, suggests declining values for males age 0 through 20 over the years 1710–1739 and a recovery 1740–1749:

Decade	N	Mean Value	Mean Age
1710–1719	13	23.3	11.1
1720–1729	30	15.1	10.0
1730–1739	15	12.1	6.1
1740–1749	43	20.4	9.0

But such a conclusion ignores the falling, then rising, mean age of the group. A general *upward* trend in values is suggested by partial correlation coefficients—value on date holding age constant—of 0.47 (male) and 0.5 (female), both significant at the 0.001 level

11. The 5% inflation between 1700 and 1723 specified is based upon an examination of evaluations of infants less than or equal to two years of age. We assume that confounding elements in the evaluation process would be minimal for this age group. The weakest infants would die within the first month of life, hence have little chance of entry into our sample; differences in strength and endurance which might catch an evaluator's eye and cause him to raise or lower the value of a child or adolescent would not yet be visible. The 49% inflation between 1723 and 1745 has been adopted from P.M.G. Harris's Maryland price series as reported by Clemens, *Atlantic Economy*, 228. The actual deflator is defined as

$$1 - (0.329 * ((Y - 1723) / 22)))$$

where Y (the year of the inventory) is greater than or equal to 1723 and

$$1 + (-0.053 * ((Y - 1723) / 23)))$$

where Y lies between 1699 and 1723. Using deflated values in the regression results in regression lines defined by intercepts and slopes of 3.108 and 1.289 (male) and 2.203 and 1.241 (female). At the same time the predictive (or estimating) power of the regression (r-squared) improves to 0.89 (females) and 0.81 (males).

12. Specifically $(12.6 - 2.203) / 1.241 = 8.3$

13. Our most appropriate choices were the mean or one standard deviation above or below the mean. The last two would bias the final result toward an older or younger population respectively. We selected one standard deviation above and accepted the upward bias.

14. Middlesex Wills, 1713–1734, 360.

15. The fitting was accomplished using the polynomial regression program (BMDP52 as revised through December 1977) developed at the Health Sciences Computing Facility, University of California at Los Angeles under the sponsorship of the National Institute of Health's Special Research Resources Grant RR-3.

16. The initial cargo of the simulation was set to match that described by Kulikoff, "'Prolifick' People," *South. Stud.*, XVI (1977), 399 as "typical." In the absence of any stronger numbers, we used age-specific mortality and fertility rates derived from Middlesex whites as described above under "Mortality" and "Fertility," suppressing the malarial bulge imparted to white female mortality. Seasoning was simulated by exaggerating first-year mortality five-fold. The low African fertility suggested by both Kulikoff (ibid., 398–401) and Russell R. Menard, "The Maryland Slave Population, 1658 to 1730: A Demographic Profile of Blacks in Four Counties," *WMQ*, 3d Ser., XXXII (1975), 38–42 was approximated by reducing the fertility of the females in the cargo generally by 30% and applying full fertility rates only to their female descendants. Both Menard and Kulikoff suggest that the initial African population could not sustain itself demographically and actually declined, necessitating further importations. The simulation indicates otherwise. Only if black mortality appreciably exceeded white mortality or African fertility were depressed to an even greater extent than either suggests would the population have shown a significant drop.

17. We have isolated the portions of the population hardest hit by epidemics by aggregating all deaths during an epidemic year (or years) and for an equal period before and after the epidemic, breaking deaths by age and sex, then computing the percent of the total in each category occurring during the epidemic period itself. For example: The susceptibility of black children to the epidemic of 1721 shows when we aggregate all black deaths at ages 0 through 9 for 1720, 1721, and 1722 and compute the percent of this aggregation dying in 1721. Normally one would expect a result of roughly 33%. A departure from normality greater than 10% implies to us a condition of abnormality, that is, an epidemic afflicting the age group. The results:

| | Age Group | | | Sex | |
	0-9	10-19	20+	Male	Female
% Deaths 1720-1722 Occurring 1721	50.0	30.0	36.8	40.0	47.8
% Deaths 1723-1731 Occurring 1726-1728	33.8	54.5	50.0	46.2	40.7
% Deaths 1736-1738 Occurring 1737	52.9	83.3	66.6	61.9	62.5

18. When the 1698-1702 descriptions are broken into five-year age groups the echoes of two earlier importations are very clear. The 25-29 group encompasses 33.7% of the total, the 35-39 group 5.5% (to be contrasted with 4.5% for 30-34). Given the importance of Wormeley and Willis inventories of 1701 in establishing this group of descriptions, the bulges in the age profile suggest major importations of blacks in 1684 and 1696.

19. The low overall sex ratio (1.1) is in contrast to the ratios for the groups isolated in note 18 as probable residues of significant importations in 1684 and 1696 (1.5 and 1.3 respectively). The sex ratio of all age groups excluding 25-29 and 30-34 was 1.0. There is some indication that planters such as Willis and Wormeley sought to pair their mature slaves.

20. Notably in his "The Beginnings of the Afro-American Family in Maryland," Land, et al., eds., *Law. Society and Politics in Early Maryland.*, 171-196, and "The Origins of Afro-American Society in Tidewater Maryland and Virginia, 1700 to 1790," *WMQ*, 3d Ser., XXXV (1978), 226-259.

21. Menard, "Maryland Slave Population," *WMQ*, 3d Ser., XXXII (1975), 29-54 based his study on inventories of four Maryland counties. Relying solely on inventories, he was frequently unable to establish the sex of his subjects while his estimates of age were to a large extent intuitive and unsystematic--"some educated guesswork," he called it (p. 31). Kulikoff, "'Prolific' People," *South. Stud.*, XVI (1977), 390-428 drew on Menard but added important qualitative evidence from county and plantation records. Nevertheless, there is essential agreement between their studies and ours.

22. The simulation involved simply the application of production and cost factors to the basic demographic model already described. We applied the age-value curve of figure 35 to arrive at the initial cost of the cargo and current capital as represented by the slave force in any given year. Because the curve depicts prices in 1723, we effectively standardized capitalization at a 1723 base. We set productivity of a male, age 16 through 39, at 1,200 pounds of tobacco, age 40-49 at 900 pounds, age 10-15 and 50-59 at 600, reducing productivity in these age categories by 25% for females, and assumed no production from children 0-9 and adults 60 and over. The 1,200 pound crop is demonstrably high for Middlesex, but we used it in an attempt to encompass the value of the slaves' labor apart from tobacco. In converting productivity to pounds current (in effect establishing gross income from slave capital) we held tobacco prices constant to the level of 1723. We set costs (the annual maintenance of a slave) as a constant to reflect the base, viz.: food per adult male and female, 26s current, clothing, medical care and the like, 11s 6d, levy 9s. The cost of children 10-15 was set at 72% of the cost of an adult, children 0-9 at 42%. Additionally, we assumed an

overseer for every 10 adults and added 23.4*s* to the annual cost of each (one-tenth of one-and-one-half crops converted to current money). Specific sources rationalize these figures. Thus Stiverson and Butler, eds., "Journal of William Hugh Grove," *Va. Mag. Hist. Biog.*, LXXXV (1977), 32, supplies us with our food costs. The MS Account Book of John Tayloe, 1714–1723, Tayloe Papers, Virginia Historical Society, Richmond, and a number of guardianship accounts from Middlesex (that covering John Seager's inheritance in Middlesex Wills, 1740–1748, 163–167, for example) suggest the clothing and miscellaneous costs. Many documents delineate the overseer's share, but see the particularly full agreement in Francis Lewis Berkeley, Jr., "The Berkeleys of Barn Elms, Planters of Colonial Virginia and a Calendar of the Berkeley Papers," (M.A. Thesis, University of Virginia, 1940), 77–78. Our production differential on the basis of age follows from the Tobacco Acts of 1723 and 1728 in Winfree, comp., *Supplement to Hening*, 247–253, 295–305, and on the various actions of the county court in declaring elderly slaves levy-free, that is to say, unproductive.

23. Clemens, *Atlantic Economy*, 151–156 addresses some of the same questions we do using other methods and factors. Unfortunately, his computations are predicated solely on the cost and production of a prime male surviving through his working years, hence his conclusions are neither entirely comparable nor particularly realistic. Where our approaches can be compared we are in rough agreement. For example, the net annual profit of a prime male slave working without an overseer and producing oronoco in Talbot County, Maryland in 1720 was about 4.8*ℓi* Maryland current or 3.6*ℓi* sterling, according to Clemens's calculations. The same slave producing sweetscented in Middlesex at the same time netted approximately 4.5*ℓi* sterling or 4.1 when the oronoco-sweetscented price differential is taken into account.

List of Tables and Figures

Tables

Figures

Figures

Figures

Index